SOUTHERN
RAILWAY GALLERY

A PICTORIAL JOURNEY THROUGH TIME

In memory of Colin George Bright,
5 November 1954 – 27April 2013.
A good friend, professional railwayman and
lifelong transport enthusiast.

SOUTHERN RAILWAY GALLERY

A PICTORIAL JOURNEY THROUGH TIME

JOHN SCOTT-MORGAN

PEN & SWORD
TRANSPORT

First published in Great Britain in 2017 by
Pen & Sword Transport

An imprint of Pen & Sword Books Ltd
47 Church Street, Barnsley South Yorkshire S70 2AS

ISBN 9781473855793

Pen & Sword Books Ltd incorporates the imprints of Pen & Sword Archaeology, Atlas, Aviation, Battleground, Discovery, Family History, History, Maritime, Military, Naval, Politics, Railways, Select, Social History, Transport, True Crime, and Claymore Press, Frontline Books, Leo Cooper, Praetorian Press, Remember When, Seaforth Publishing and Wharncliffe.

For a complete list of Pen & Sword titles please contact
Pen & Sword Books Limited
47 Church Street, Barnsley, South Yorkshire, S70 2AS, England
E-mail: enquiries@pen-and-sword.co.uk
Website: www.pen-and-sword.co.uk

Printed and bound by Replika Press Pvt. Ltd

INTRODUCTION

The Southern Railway was the smallest of the big four railways, that came into being on the 1 January 1923. The grouping of Britain's railways caused a lot of anxiety among the officers and staff of the various companies concerned, where old rivalries and distrust between companies often continued into the new era of the amalgamated big four.

The Southern Railway was made up of four main companies:

The London & South Western operated from Waterloo to Portsmouth via Guildford, with a main line that also linked the capital with Weymouth via Southampton and Bournemouth. A large part of the L&SWR was in the West Country, serving Somerset, Dorset, Devon and North Cornwall, a long way from the bustling metropolis of London or the rolling hills of Hampshire. It was to all intents and purposes the senior partner in the Southern group, having some of the most prestigious trains and most up to date motive power. It had already started to electrify its London suburban network in 1915, using a DC third rail system, with the line from Waterloo to Wimbledon via Putney.

The London Brighton & South Coast Railway, on the other hand, operated a more sedate network, running out of London Bridge and Victoria to places in Surrey, East and West Sussex, parts of western Kent and parts of east Hampshire. Like the L&SWR, the LB&SCR also had a good modern fleet of express Locomotives, some fine carriage stock and a well-maintained fleet of freight vehicles. It was also slowly introducing electrification on its London suburban lines with the operation of an AC overhead system on the South London line from London Bridge to Victoria, which the company intended to extend to Crystal Palace and eventually the main line to Brighton.

The weakest links in the main line railways taken into the new Southern group was in the form of the South Eastern Railway and the London Chatham & Dover Railway, which had formed a joint management committee in 1899, in order to end the negative rivalry that had existed between the two companies since the Victorian era. The Southern Railway had to negotiate two separate agreements with the companies concerned, in order to take over them both.

The South Eastern & Chatham Railway Joint Committee operated railways in Kent and along the East Sussex border, serving the towns along the Medway, the Channel ports of Dover and Folkestone and the holiday destinations in Thanet and the East Sussex coast from Rye to Hastings. It served the East Kent coal field and also the cement industry in North Kent, which provided the railway with through freight traffic to other main line railways via London and its Tonbridge to Reading line. It was planning to electrify its South London suburban network, at the time of the 1923 grouping, however the company planned to use a different system of DC third rail pick up to that of the L&SWR, with its conductor rails in a different position. As the SE&CR electrification project had not progressed by the time of the grouping, the newly formed Southern Railway was able to abandon the scheme and substitute it with the L&SWR third rail pick up system. The SE&CR was the church mouse in the Southern group, in that it was the least well off railway vested in the new company, with the least modern Locomotives and rolling stock.

The Southern Railway was, from very early on, a great believer and investor in electric traction, not only electrifying its London suburban services but also converting at an early stage much of its main line operations on the former Brighton system, electrifying the main line from Victoria and London Bridge to Brighton, Eastbourne and Hastings, all of which was achieved between 1933-1936.

On the former L&SWR, the company electrified the suburban network in South West London and out as far as Alton in 1935, continuing with the main line electrification of the Portsmouth Direct in 1937. There were plans in the late 1930s, to electrify the main line network in Kent, but the Second World War intervened, curtailing these plans until British Railways days, in the late 1950s and early 1960s.

All four railways brought shipping companies to the Southern group, which were vested in the Channel Packet Company, the Southern's shipping company. Along with the railways themselves, the newly formed Southern Railway, inherited a number of docks and harbours, from the Kent coast to North Devon and Cornwall.

In addition to the main line constituents, the Southern also took over some interesting small railways: the Plymouth Devonport & South Western Junction Railway, which operated an independent line between Bere Alston and Callington, with running rights to Plymouth; and the narrow gauge Lynton & Barnstaple Light Railway, in North Devon. In truth, one could say that the Lynton & Barnstaple Light Railway, was a missed opportunity, in that, unlike the Great Western, who made the most of owning the Vail of Rheidol Light Railway in mid Wales, the Southern never really understood this little gem of a railway, which could have made a tidy profit for the company from tourist traffic, had it been properly advertised and promoted.

An interesting development in North Devon and Cornwall at this time was the construction and opening in 1925 of the North Devon & Cornwall Junction Railway, a line from Halwill Junction to Torrington, which connected two important Ex L&SWR routes, at the far end of the Southern system. The ND&CJR, was always an independent railway, with a separate management based in an office in London, at Waterloo station; it was not taken over until nationalisation in 1948, when it became part of the Southern Region of British Railways, the chief Engineer for the project being Colonel Holman Fred Stephens, the famous light railway Engineer and railway administrator.

The Southern also absorbed three small railways on the Isle of Wight, these being the Isle of Wight Railway, from Ryde Pier Head to Ventnor, with a branch to Bembridge; the Isle of Wight Central, from Ryde St Johns Road to Cowes, via Newport, with a cross country line to Shanklin and a branch to Ventnor West; and the Freshwater Yarmouth & Newport Railway, which was a small almost bankrupt concern, operating a short branch from Newport to Freshwater, in the western extremity of the Island. The Island's railways were put into the able hands of AB McCloud, who made bricks without straw, by managing the Island network with skill, turning a sow's ear into a silk purse.

As a result of electrification projects on the London suburban network, McCloud was able to acquire almost new steam non-corridor carriage stock and more modern redundant tank Locomotives, for use on the Island system. Thus, thirty-six Ex-L&SWR, 02 0-4-4 tanks and four Ex-LB&SCR, E1 0-6-0 tanks were shipped to the Island, along with a large number of Brighton and South Eastern & Chatham bogie carriage stock. In addition to this, three redundant Brighton A1 X Terrier class 0-6-0 tank locomotives, also gravitated across the Solent for use on the Island's branch lines, supplementing members of the same class, inherited from the grouped Isle of Wight Central and Freshwater Yarmouth & Newport Railway.

The influx of good second hand locomotives and rolling stock enabled AB McCloud to withdraw a large amount of old worn out equipment and rejuvenate the whole system. During the mid-1920s and early 1930s the network on the Island was transformed from a rundown ramshackle affair to a smart, efficient, business-like concern, with brightly painted Locomotives and rolling stock, well-kept stations and a punctual time table. AB McCloud introduced many new innovations and features to the Island railways, including the enlarged coal bunkers on the 02 tanks and a naming policy, which reflected the places to visit on the Island.

The Southern Railway also took a controlling interest in the Vectis Bus Company, which became Southern Vectis, thus taking over the railway's main rival form of transport on the Island. In addition, the company had a controlling interest in the Southern National Bus Company, which operated services in parts of the West Country. It was not only on the Isle of Wight that things needed to be improved, but also on the main line and branch network on the mainland, where lack of investment and the Great War had taken its toll.

Much of the permanent way and infrastructure was in need of attention and renewal, especially in Kent, where sea shale ballast was used by the SE&CR, as a cheap form of packing for its track. After the Sevenoaks disaster in 1927, when a boat train derailed near Pollyhill Tunnel, causing much loss of life, the whole main line network in Kent had to be re-ballasted using Meldon granite ballast, to replace the poor quality material from Dungeness

The new company had an interesting and diverse selection of Locomotives and rolling stock, as well as an equally diverse portfolio of structures and civil engineering across the network.

One of the more unfortunate consequences in the early years of the company was the reaction of ill-informed journalists and politicians who often made stupid comments in the papers and parliament which at times led to the company being the butt of music hall jokes. Sir Herbert Walker, the railway's general manager, tackled this problem by employing John Elliot, a journalist from Fleet Street, to set up a press and public relations department. As a result of this new department being set up, the whole public image of the Southern Railway changed and a more positive outlook prevailed, over a short period of time.

It was John Elliott who was responsible for the naming policy of the Southern Locomotives, starting with the King Arthur class 4-6-0 tender passenger Locomotives in 1925. Richard Maunsell, the companies Chief Mechanical Engineer, remarked to Elliott at the time, 'It won't make them run any faster'; perhaps that was true, but the public and press loved the naming of large impressive express Locomotives.

The Southern started to name some of its long distance express trains, these included the Atlantic Coast Express, the Bournemouth Belle and the Southern Belle, which later after electrification, became the Brighton Belle. This was followed post war in 1947, with the introduction of the Devon Belle and lastly the Thanet Belle. This provided the passengers who travelled on the Southern with a high standard of luxury travel, not always afforded by the other big four companies.

To many people, the Southern became the holiday line, a railway that took you from the smoky city to the countryside and more importantly, to the coast. The company had forward-looking advertising to entice passengers to the seaside and the far away hills for holidays and weekend trips. Sunny South Sam, with his warm smile, would look down on commuters and other travellers, from giant hoardings at stations and along the line, encouraging them to go Southern or Southern Electric.

During the 1930s, the company had come into its own, with ever growing passenger numbers and improved train services, an aspect of ongoing improvement from this period being the reconstruction of a number of stations and other buildings in reinforced concrete, often referred to as the Walker period buildings. These buildings and structures were loosely based on designs being constructed by London Transport, for the Underground and their bus network. The concrete was a by-product, using granite stone dust from the company's quarry at Meldon, near Oakhampton in North Devon. The Southern Railway established a concrete works near Exmouth Junction, to produce prefabricated concrete products, anything from fence posts to complete footbridges and line side huts. This style of architecture became a hallmark of the Southern Railway and was carried on well into British Railways days. It was the Second World War that prevented further expansion of this policy and curtailed further improvements, including extensions to the electrified network.

Richard Maunsell, the Southern's Chief Mechanical Engineer, inherited a very mixed bag of Locomotives and rolling stock, with some equipment and motive power dating back to the mid-nineteenth century. He had designed locomotives for the South Eastern & Chatham Railway, before being appointed as Chief Mechanical Engineer of the Southern Railway in 1923. Although the company decided to electrify its London suburban lines, shortly after the grouping in 1923, there was also a growing case for the electrification of main lines in Sussex, Kent and parts of Eastern Hampshire, the justification being a saving on staff and costs if steam traction was replaced with clean modern electric traction in these areas, not too far from London. There was

a clear need to provide modern efficient steam motive power, as a stop gap in the short, or medium term, until finance allowed for long distance electrification schemes to take place.

As a result of this, Richard Maunsell, designed a series of new main line steam Locomotives to replace a whole host of old and worn out types, beginning with the continuation of the construction of Urie N 15, 4-6-0s, fitted with Maunsell boilers in 1925 and the order placed with the North British Locomotive Company of further batches of new King Arthur 4-6-0s, the Scotch Arthurs.

The next large Locomotive development, the introduction of the sixteen Lord Nelson 4-6-0 tender express Locomotives, came about in 1926. These impressive looking machines were designed to haul the most important express trains on the Southern system, including the Southampton boat trains and top link turns to Exeter, on the former L&SWR West of England main line. The Lord Nelsons were also to be found hauling the boat trains to Dover and Folkestone, including the all-Pullman, Golden Arrow. The Lord Nelson 4-6-0s left a lot to be desired when it came to free steaming and underwent many modifications over the decades, right through to British Railways days; both Richard Maunsell and Oliver Bulleid, attempted to improve the steaming of these large Locomotives, with mixed results.

In 1931, the Schools class V 4-4-0s were introduced, which were probably the finest and best Locomotives ever designed by Richard Maunsell, a modest sized 4-4-0, with the power of a King Arthur 4-6-0, these neat 4-4-0 tender Locomotives were constructed to provide modern motive power for trains on the Hastings line, but also found themselves on main line services elsewhere in Sussex and Kent, as well as doing turns on the South Western main line.

There was also a need for new mixed traffic and freight Locomotives, this again was provided by Maunsell and his team, in the form of the family of 2-6-0s, the two cylinder N and the three cylinder N1, classes and the two cylinder U and three cylinder U1 classes. These successful Mogul types were introduced from 1923 and large numbers of the two cylinder types were constructed, including a sizable number from Woolwich Arsenal, constructed after the end of World War One. Of all the classes of Locomotive to be found across the whole Southern network, the Maunsell Moguls were probably the only class one could find in every area, the railway served.

Less successful were the ill-fated River K class 2-6-4 tanks, which used a large number of parts from the Mogul-type Locomotives. Like the Moguls, the tank Locomotives came in two versions; the two cylinder K class and a single example as a three cylinder type, the K 1 class. These handsome express 2-6-4 tanks, suffered from instability while travelling at high speed on the Southern's poorly ballasted track in Kent and parts of Sussex. After a number of near accidents involving members of the class nearly jumping off the track on express passenger trains, a member of the class finally derailed at high speed near Sevenoaks in the summer of 1927, while hauling a boat train, killing thirteen and seriously injuring 132 passengers and destroying a wooden bodied Pullman Car. In subsequent tests held independently on the London & North Eastern Railway, it was found that the K class 2-6-4 tanks, were steady at high speed and the design was not to blame; however, the damage was done and all members of the class were rebuilt as U class, 2-6-0 tender Locomotives as a result.

As part of the ongoing improvements to the Locomotive fleet, Richard Maunsell also introduced the L 1 4-4-0s in 1926, for use on passenger services in Kent; the Z class 0-8-0 tanks introduced in 1929, for heavy shunting in marshalling yards; the W class 2-6-4 tanks, introduced in 1931, for heavy freight transfer work; and the Q

class 0-6-0 tender goods, in 1938, to replace older freight Locomotives. He was also responsible for ordering three 0-6-0 diesel mechanical shunters in 1938, for use at Norwood Yard in South London.

In 1937, Richard Maunsell officially retired as Chief Mechanical Engineer, making way for Oliver Bulleid, who had been principal assistant to Sir Nigel Gresley, on the L&NER.

Bulleid had a very different view of Locomotive and rolling stock design to Richard Maunsell, introducing some of the most radical and controversial Locomotives in British railway history. At the time Bulleid took over in 1937, the Q class 0-6-0 tender goods was being introduced, a design he regarded as being old fashioned and pedestrian.

More Q class 0-6-0s were planned, but Bulleid stopped the order and completely redesigned the machines, which resulted in the very controversial Q1 class, introduced in 1942, a very futuristic design, a mixture of pure wartime austerity and modern movement, in its concept. The 40 Q1 0-6-0s, were the most powerful tender goods locomotive ever constructed, having a tractive effort of 30,080lb, which set the class above the average machines of that wheel arrangement, at that time.

Oliver Bulleid is best remembered for his two designs of Pacifics, the thirty Merchant Navy Class, introduced in 1941 and the 110 light Pacifics, introduced in 1945. The Pacifics changed the face of the Southern's express services and were, for many, a welcome improvement on the rather staid and outdated motive power that had existed on many lines, before their introduction. Despite the restrictions that the Second World War imposed on the railways of Britain and on the Southern, which was nearest to the conflict, the company managed to get through and introduce improvements that eluded the other three 'big four' companies.

The company suffered badly from air raid damage, especially during the early part of the war, when the London Blitz and attacks on the network along the south coast disrupted train services on a regular basis. The Southern showed its best during the evacuation of the Army from the beeches at Dunkirk, operating countless trains for the surviving BEF and rescued French troops to clear the Kent ports.

Things improved after the Battle of Britain and Hitler's abandonment of the invasion of Britain, when there were fewer air raids and things settled down to a certain extent. This was a period when the company could take stock and consolidate the war time situation, before the second great onslaught, during the period in 1944 after D Day, when the South of England and London were under attack from the V weapons.

During the war the Southern, along with the other big four companies, contributed greatly to the war effort, not only in providing the military with necessary transport, but also the construction of much needed war materials, including tank landing craft, armoured vehicles and anti-aircraft guns, which were fabricated in its workshops at Ashford, Brighton and Eastleigh.

At the end of the European war, in May 1945, the Southern Railway had survived, but was in need of investment to return the system to pre-war standards. The company continued to construct and introduce new Locomotives and rolling stock, in the years from 1945-1947, with both new steam and sets of electric stock, being outshopped to Bulleid designs for main line and suburban use. Despite the Labour victory in the 1945 general election and the decision to nationalise Britain's railways, along with the other key strategic public utilities, the big four companies continued to invest and plan for the future, the Southern Railway being no exception, with its plans for double decker electric suburban trains, the Leader class bogie articulated steam Locomotive and the continuation of the construction of the two classes of Bulleid Pacifics.

Among the post war plans, which came to fruition after nationalisation, were the three type 3 Diesel Electric 1 Co- Co 1 Locomotives 10201-10203, which became the prototypes for the later British Railways, class 40. Also, as part of the ongoing modernisation of the Southern Electric motive power, two Co Co Locomotives had been constructed and introduced in 1941, these machines originally numbered CC1 and CC2, later, 20001 and 20002, were joined after nationalisation by a third modified Locomotive, number 20003, in 1951.

The Southern Railway ceased to exist as a railway operator, at midnight on the 31 December 1947, after an existence of twenty four years, during which the company had achieved much to amalgamate four main line and a host of smaller operating companies, into a cohesive, efficient operating organisation, serving an area from the Kent coast to the far reaches of Devon and North Cornwall, providing the public with a safe reliable passenger and freight service, that was in the main second to none.

John Scott-Morgan
Woking, November 2016.

ACKNOWLEDGEMENTS

I should like to thank the following, for their kind help in producing this book.
James Garratt, Milepost 92, Photomatic, Richard Stumpf, Lens of Sutton Association, R.M. Casserley, H.C. Casserley, J.H. Aston, R.K. Blencowe and LCGB Ken Nunn Collection.
I have endeavoured to contact every copyright holder of pictures for this book; however, if I have left anyone out, I apologise and please contact me through the publishers.

Ex South Eastern & Chatham Railway Q Class 0-4-4T, number 173, heads a train of Ex-London Chatham & Dover four wheeled carriage stock, on a London area suburban train c.1923. This picture shows the type of trains that were being operated in early Southern days, on some parts of the network, before suburban electrification. (R.C. Stumpf Collection)

An Ex S E & C R Q1 class 0-4-4 T, number 12, heads a train of Ex S E & C R non-corridor carriage stock, on an outer suburban service, operating from the London suburbs to eastern border with Kent, c.1925; already the conductor rails are in position, ready for electric traction.
(R.C. Stumpf Collection)

Waterloo Terminus, on the London & South Western Railway, c.1923, with Drummond T9, 4-4-0, number 297, awaiting departure with an express service. A proportion of these Locomotives had been rebuilt by Robert Urie; by this time, however, the newly formed Southern continued into the 1920s to rebuild the rest of this successful class. (R.C. Stumpf Collection)

London Brighton & South Coast Railway I 3 4-4-2T heads a train of Pullmans through the suburbs, with a fast service from Victoria to Brighton c.1923. The LBSCR was a great user of Pullman cars, especially on the services to Brighton, which had a booked timing of an hour, from London to the coast. (R.C. Stumpf Collection)

An Ex-SE&CR Stirling F class 4-4-0, number 172, double heads with a Wainwright C Class 0-6-0 tender goods, heading an excursion train to the Kent coast c 1925. A number of Stirling F class 4-4-0 tender Locomotives, were still in original condition, at the time of the grouping in 1923; a large proportion of the class were rebuilt by Wainwright becoming F1 class, in the 1900s. (R.C. Stumpf Collection)

South Eastern Central and South Western Divisions

Ex S E & C R, F 1 4-4-0 tender Locomotive number 1002, heads for the inky blackness of St Leonards Warrior Square Tunnel, on 5 October 1933, with a train for London. Although by this time the Southern was constructing new modern steam Locomotive classes to replace older Victorian and Edwardian machines, most of the railways services still relied on older motive power to operate some of its main line services. (H.C. Casserley)

Interlude at Tonbridge Wells, West station, on the former LBSCR, 18 May 1936, with D 3 0-4-4 T, number 2580, about to depart with a local stopping service. Tonbridge Wells, had two stations at this time; Central, on the Hastings line, formally SE&CR and the west station, formally LBSCR. (H.C. Casserley)

Schools class number 901 Winchester, speeds a London bound train through Wadhurst on 18 May 1936. The Schools class became the main top link Locomotive on the Hastings line after their introduction, replacing the earlier inside cylinder 4-4-0 classes on the more important services. (H.C. Casserley)

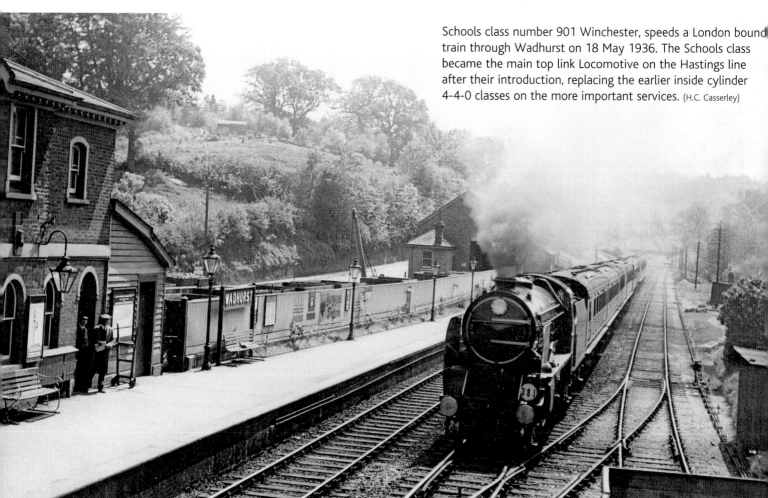

H class 0-4-4 T, number 1305, stands in the platform at Lenham, with a local stopping service from Ashford to Maidstone East c.1947. The Locomotive is quite clean in its wartime black livery, with just a dusting of grime, on its paint work. (R.C. Stumpf Collection)

Ex S E & C R D Class 4-4-0, number 1737, heads a train through the Warren, between Dover and Folkestone c.1936. This section of line was closed for most of the First World War, owing to a substantial land slip which derailed a passenger train and blocked the line. (Rev Mace, Milepost 92)

An F 1 4-4-0 tender Locomotive No. 1060 departs Ramsgate station with a semi-fast train of Ex-SE&CR Bird Cadge stock to London, c.1935. This picture shows the station and carriage shed clearly; the Locomotive shed can just be seen on the far left. (Rev Mace, Milepost 92)

Schools class 4-4-0s running neck and neck, between Hither Green and Grove Park. Numbers 900 ETON and 906 Sherborne are shown in this 1935 picture. The Schools class 4-4-0 tender Locomotives were the mainstay of many of the express passenger services in Kent and parts of Sussex, during the 1930s and 1940s, only being ousted by dieselisation in the late 1950s. (Rev Mace, Milepost 92)

An L1 4-4-0 number 1753 departs Dover Marine, with a train of Maunsell carriage stock bound for London c 1936, passing the Lord Walden Hotel on its way out of the town. The L1 4-4-0s were introduced in March 1926, being a follow on to the other Maunsell inspired inside cylinder 4-4-0s and like them spent most of their working lives in Kent and Sussex. (Rev Mace, Milepost 92)

Wainwright H class tank, number 1239, stands in the centre road at Deal c.1936, with a train of Ex-SE&CR Bird Cage carriage stock. The H class tanks worked local services along the Kent coast and were also used on many branch lines in Kent and Sussex. (Milepost 92)

Bulleid Light Pacific 21C140, later named *Crewkerne,* stands in the platform at Dover Marine station in the summer of 1948. These light Pacifics, introduced in 1945, became the main top link Locomotives on the Southern Railway and later British Railways, Southern Region, 110 examples being constructed from 1945 to 1951, when production of big four-designed Locomotive types ceased. (Rev Mace, Milepost 92)

A pair of Ex-SE&CR R1 0-6-0 tanks, numbers 1337 and 1174, haul a boat train out of Folkestone Harbour station c.1936. These old, but reliable tank Locomotives survived in traffic until 1960, when the final example was withdrawn from service, being replaced at Folkestone with Ex-Great Western 57XX pannier tanks. (Rev Mace, Milepost 92)

King Arthur N15 4-6-0 number 763 *Sir Bors de Ganis,* heads a Ramsgate to Victoria train, near Dumpton Park, on 20 May 1939. This is an interesting train formation, with Maunsell carriage stock and a Pullman dining car. (Rev Mace, Milepost 92)

An Ex-SE&CR F1 4-4-0 runs through Chilworth station with a semi fast service on 21 March 1936. The F1 and D class 4-4-0 tender Locomotives provided most of the main motive power for the passenger services at this time. The Reading, Tonbridge line, was and still is an important strategic route, connecting the west of England and the Midlands with the Kent and Sussex coast. (H.C. Casserley)

Ex-LBSCR K class 2-6-0, number 345, heads a cross country passenger service down the Brighton main line c.1930. The K class Moguls, were some of the most successful modern LBSCR Locomotives ever constructed, seeing service until December 1962. (Author's Collection)

H 2 Brighton Atlantic number 2421, South Foreland, emerges from Lewes tunnel, with a boat train for New Haven Harbour c.1935. (Author's Collection)

H 1 Brighton Atlantic number 2038 Portland Bill, stands in the platform at Newhaven Harbour on 11 October 1933. These beautiful Atlantic Locomotives were a feature on the Newhaven Boat trains until the mid-1950s, when the last H2 examples were withdrawn. A replica Brighton Atlantic is currently being constructed at the Bluebell Railway in East Sussex. (H.C. Casserley)

Ex-LBSCR E5 0-6-2T, number 593, poses for the camera, next to a permanent way gang, near Horsham in the early 1930s; note the conductor rails are being made ready to energise and steam passenger services will soon be a thing of the past. (Author's Collection)

A Marsh, Brighton Radial tank number B 30, storms through Arundel station, with an express on 10 October 1932. At the time of the formation of the Southern Railway in 1923, the three main groups of former pre-grouping companies' Locomotives were renumbered, using an area letter to designate origin, Ex-SE&CR being A, for Ashford; Ex-LBSCR, being B for Brighton; Ex-L&SWR being E for Eastleigh; and Isle of Wight being W. This arrangement later changed with the introduction of an extra digit to each number, giving the Locomotives four digit numbers. (H.C. Casserley)

Ex L B S C R B4X 4-4-0 tender Locomotive number 52, heads an express service, made up of mixed bogie carriage stock c 1926. These sturdy express passenger Locomotives, provided modern motive power for many of the Victoria Brighton fast trains in the 1920s and early 1930s. A number of these reliable machines, were to see service until the first years of British Railways, the last not being withdrawn until the early 1950s. O J Morris

Ex-L&SWR T 9 4-4-0, number 310, arrives at Lewes station in the summer of 1936, with a train for Eastbourne. During the mid to late 1930s, the Southern cascaded more modern 4-4-0s from the Western division to the Eastern and Central divisions, in order to replace older 4-4-0 types that were due for withdrawal. The former south western Locomotives, were equipped with six wheeler tenders, so they could be turned on the smaller turn tables on the Eastern and Central divisions. (Rev Mace, Milepost 92)

An Ex-LBSCR Stroudley D1 0-4-2 T, lurks in the shadows as Billington E3, 0-6-2T number 2167, simmers in the sunshine at Lewes station in the summer of 1936. The vehicle next to the E3 tank is of interest, being a LBSCR horsebox. (Rev Mace, Milepost 92)

A local train departs Lewes in the summer of 1935, headed by a Stroudley D1 0-4-2 tank, hauling Ex Brighton and a solitary SE&CR carriage, next to the Locomotive. (Rev Mace, Milepost 92)

Ex-LBSCR E2 0-6-0 T, number 103, shunts carriage stock at Forest Hill, c.1923. These powerful Brighton 0-6-0 tank Locomotives, were originally used on passenger and outer suburban services; however, owing to electrification in the London area, they quickly gravitated to other duties, including pilot work and shunting at marshalling yards. (Rev Mace, Milepost 92)

Stroudley D1 0-4-2T, number 356, makes ready to leave Eastbourne station with a local stopping train in the summer of 1926. The D1 class were versatile tank Locomotives that lasted in traffic for most of the twenty-four years of the Southern's existence. Some members of the class were modified during the Second World War for use as firefighting pumps and one became a pumping engine, for refuelling oil-burning Locomotives in 1947. (Rev Mace, Milepost 92)

H2 Brighton Atlantic 2423, The Needles, runs through Honour Oak, with an express train, made up of Maunsell corridor stock and a solitary Pullman car, providing a restaurant service, c.1935. (Rev Mace, Milepost 92)

Ex L & S W R M7 0-4-4 T number 132, heads a stopping train of South Western Panter non-corridor carriage stock, on the Waterloo Reading line c 1930. (R.C. Stumpf

Drummond D15 4-4-0, number 467, speeds an up Portsmouth to London service, through Liphook station on 21 March 1936. The D15 4-4-0s were the last design produced by Dougal Drummond being introduced in 1912 and were later rebuilt by Robert Urie, during the First World War. These Locomotives hauled the main line expresses on the Portsmouth line until largely replaced, by the Schools class 4-4-0s in the early 1930s. (H.C. Casserley)

D15 4-4-0, number 463, passes Southcote Junction, with a passenger service to Basingstoke c.1930. The train is made up of Ex-L&SWR Panter non-corridor carriage stock, which was widely used on these services at this time. (M.W. Earley)

Schools class 4-4-0, number 926, Repton, starts away from Guildford, with an up express from Portsmouth to Waterloo, c.1935. This view shows how extensive the goods yard was at this important junction, also how much freight and coal traffic was once handled there. (Rev Mace, Milepost 92)

Ex-L&SWR Adams X2 4-4-0 number 583, heads a semi fast passenger train near Bournemouth on 9 May 1925. The locomotives, designed by William Adams, were well designed and long lived, some classes lasting into the mid-1960s, on British Railways. The last Adams T3 4-4-0s lasted until just after the Second World War, not being withdrawn until 1946; luckily, one example has been preserved in the national collection, number 579. (H.C. Casserley)

Urie H15 4-6-0 number 524 heads a Bournemouth express service near Fleet, on 12 May 1935. The L&SWR Urie-designed 4-6-0 classes were some of the finest Locomotives on the Southern Railway and were well liked by the foot plate crews. Most of these machines lasted well into British Railways days, not being withdrawn until the early 1960s. (R.C. Stumpf collection)

After the Brighton line was electrified in 1933 and the line to Eastbourne in 1935, a question arose over the future of the LBSCR Lawson Billington designed Baltic 4-6-4 tanks. The Locomotives were too new to scrap and had many years of life left in them; Richard Maunsell rebuilt the large tanks as useful 4-6-0 tender Locomotives, becoming N15 X and finding a new life on the South Western division. Here we see N15 X 4-6-0, number 2330, *Cudworth*, on an express near Fleet in June 1946, painted in its Bulleid wartime black livery. (R.C. Stumpf collection)

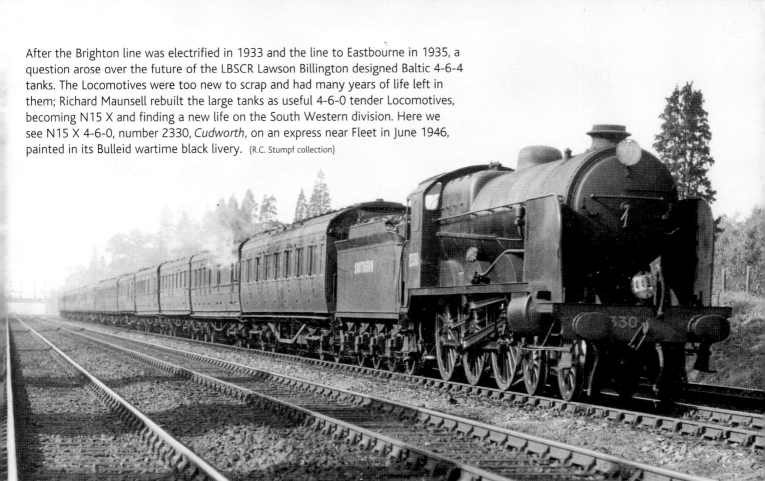

Lord Nelson 4-6-0, number 859, *Lord Hood* runs through Fleet, with special extra working to Bournemouth, made up of mixed bogie carriage stock, on 2 April 1946. In this picture, the Locomotive is in clean war time black livery, with Bulleid sun shine yellow and green shaded lettering.

Bulleid Merchant Navy Pacific number 21C10, *Blue Star*, storms through Basingstoke, with a down West of England express, in the summer of 1946. The Merchant Navy class was introduced in 1941, only ten being constructed during the Second World War, the other twenty having to wait until the post war era.
(Author's Collection)

Express Passenger Trains

Ex-LBSCR, Baltic tank number 333 Remembrance, makes an impressive sight as it speeds out of London with a boat train to Newhaven Harbour in 1928. The Baltic tanks were the main motive power on the fast Brighton and Eastbourne expresses until electrification during the mid-1930s. The overhead catenary is part of the Brighton overhead electric suburban network, which operated from Victoria to London Bridge, on the South London line and also ran out to Crystal Palace. All the Brighton Baltic tanks were later re built as 4-6-0 tender Locomotives, becoming class N15 X and being given names of Locomotive Engineers. (Author's Collection)

Prototype River Class 2-6-4 Tank number 790, River Avon, on the quarry line, with the Southern Belle Pullman express c 1925. The River K Class were introduced by the S E & C R in 1915, with this solitary example, further construction not commencing until after the First World War, was over, when a further twenty examples, were added to the class, including a single three cylinder K1 machine, number 890 River Frome constructed in 1925. All twenty one members of the class were reconstructed into 2-6-0 tender Locomotives, after the Sevenoaks disaster in 1927, when number 800 River Cray, derailed at speed near Pollyhill tunnel, with much loss of life. Authors Collection

King Arthur Class 4-6-0 tender Locomotive number 764 Sir Gawain, constructed by North British Locomotive Company in Glasgow in 1925 and is seen when new heading a boat train to the Kent coast, c1926. The Maunsell designed King Arthurs constructed in Glasgow, were always referred to as Scotch Arthurs, to differentiate them from the earlier Urie and Maunsell, Eastleigh constructed machines. Authors Collection

Scotch Arthur number 764 Sir Gawain, emerges from Shakespeare Cliff tunnel, with a boat train for Dover c.1935. Note the six wheel tender, as used on the South Eastern and Central divisions, so that these 4-6-0 tender Locomotives could be turned on smaller turntables. (Author's Collection)

Urie H15 4-6-0 number 524 heads an express through Vauxhall on 27 August 1932. This picture shows the Locomotive in its original condition, with its Urie smokebox door and other L&SWR features; these were later replaced with Maunsell fittings. (H.C. Casserley)

Lord Nelson 4-6-0 number 863 *Lord Rodney*, heads a boat express near Bromley on 26 February 1939. This Locomotive is painted in the first rendering of Bulleid malachite green, with sunshine lettering, also note the experimental chimney, fitted with an improved draughting system, based on the French Lemaitre system. (H.C. Casserley)

Schools class number 901 Winchester, speeds a Margate, Folkestone to Charing Cross Pullman car express through the fields of Kent c.1936. (Rev Mace, Milepost 92)

Wainwright E class 4-4-0 tender locomotive number 1515, heads a train of Maunsell steel bodied corridor stock through the South London suburbs, on its way to the Sussex coast, c.1936. (Rev Mace, Milepost 92)

Ex-L&SWR Drummond L12, 4-4-0 number 431, runs down the Brighton main line with a passenger working, consisting of Maunsell corridor stock and a Pullman dining car, c.1936. (Rev Mace, Milepost 92)

A Waterloo to Portsmouth service, headed by Schools class number 929 Malvern, arrives at Guildford on 3 May 1937. By this time, the Portsmouth direct line was about to be energised for electric traction and the regular workings of passenger steam Locomotives, would soon come to an end. (Rev Mace, Milepost 92)

Ex-SE&CR J class 0-6-4 T, number 1599, heads out of Ramsgate, with a passenger service for London via Ashford; the train of steel bodied Maunsell corridor stock, has the obligatory Pullman dining car. There were five J class 0-6-4 tanks, constructed at Ashford Works in 1913, designed by Surtees, during Wainwright's time. These seemingly impressive machines were not a great success in traffic, having the same boiler as the H class 0-4-4 T. Despite their deficiencies, these 0-6-4 tanks lasted into British Railways days, the last not being withdrawn until 1950. (Rev Mace, Milepost 92)

Bulleid light pacific number 21C112 Launceston, near Salisbury, with a West of England express on 21 September 1946. This picture shows the Locomotive in as-constructed condition, with the original cab with narrow windows; this was later modified with the V shaped cab, which gave better vision ahead. (LCGB Ken Nunn Collection)

Another Bulleid light pacific, number 21C162, later named 17 Squadron, here seen at Shorncliffe in the autumn of 1947. Note the experimental smoke deflectors, fitted in May 1947. (Author's Collection)

Southern and Great Western joint lines

The Isle of Portland was served by a joint line operated by the former LSWR and the Great Western, which was originally mixed broad gauge and standard gauge. The line opened in stages, Weymouth to Portland in 1865 and an extension to Easton opened in 1902. The passenger service ceased in 1952, followed by freight in 1965. Here we see 02 0-4-4T, number 221 at Easton with a branch service c.1935.

The Withered Arm

Ex-L&SWR Beattie Well tank, number 0314, at Wenford Bridge with a short china clay train c.1930. Three Beattie well tank Locomotives, were retained for use on the Wenford Bridge branch, in North Cornwall. These old 2-4-0WT Locomotives were the only machines that could negotiate the sharp curves on this freight-only branch serving the china clay industry. Although the Southern tried other Locomotives on this line, including an Ex-SE&CR P class 0-6-0T, no other Locomotive type could be found that was suitable, until in British Railways days Ex-Great Western 1366 class 0-6-0 pannier tanks were allocated as a replacement. (Rev Mace, Milepost 92)

The far Westerly reaches of the Southern system, Padstow, on the North Cornwall coast c.1923. This station was the furthest you could go on a Southern passenger train and was the final destination of the Atlantic Coast Express. Here we see the station from above, showing the station and its track layout, also the fish sheds in the middle background. (Milepost 92 Collection)

A scene at Barnstaple Locomotive depot, on the 24th May 1935, with a line-up of tank Locomotives, which includes, M7 0-4-4 Tank number 34, behind which an E1R 0-6-2 Tank and a further M7 stand out of use. H C Casserley

E1R, 0-6-2 T number 96, simmers in the platform, with a local train of mixed bogie carriage stock at Bideford c.1929. The E1R class were rebuilds of Ex-LBSCR, Stroudley E1 0-6-0 tanks, which were surplus to requirements on the Central Division. In the early 1920s, there was a need for more motive power on the newly opened North Devon & Cornwall Junction Railway and also on various Ex-L&SWR lines, in Devon and North Cornwall. The three E1R 0-6-2 tanks proved successful for the tasks, they were designed for and remained in service with British Railways until the late 1950s. (Author's Collection)

London Termini

In the early days of the Southern Railway, there were many ageing classes of steam Locomotive, including the Ex-LBSCR Stroudley B1 Gladstone class Locomotives. These venerable passenger 0-4-2 tender Locomotives, dated back to the 1880s and were still operating top link trains into the early years of the twentieth century. B1 number 198, departs London Victoria, with a semi fast train on the Brighton main line c.1925; despite its age, the Locomotive is still in sound condition and sports its coat of lined Southern olive green well. (Author's Collection)

Ex-SE&CR, E1 4-4-0 tender Locomotive, number 1511, stands in the platform on the former London Chatham & Dover side at Victoria station c.1946. Victoria station was originally owned by a consortium of three companies, the LBSCR, the LC&DR and the Great Western, which all owned shares in the terminal company and had running rights into the station. The Great Western sold its shares to the Southern Railway at the grouping in 1923, retaining running rights to South Lambeth goods depot, near Battersea power station. The Southern then started to make improvements at Victoria station, including knocking a passage through the wall that separated the LBSCR side from the LC&DR part of the station. Few people today would understand the meaning of the lines in The Importance of Being Earnest, where Ernest's reply horrified Lady Bracknell, when asked where he was found – at Victoria station, Brighton side – to many Victorians, the LC&DR was beyond the pale. (Author's Collection)

Much modified Marsh I1X 4-4-2 tank number 2005, waits at the head of its train at London Bridge station c.1935. Richard Maunsell had these large Ex-LBSC R 4-4-2 tanks rebuilt to allow them greater route availability across the Southern system. The changes included shorter chimneys, lowered cab roofs and squatter dome covers. This station, which had a listed roof, has now been demolished and replaced with a new modern steel and concrete structure that pays little heed to the sights importance in London's railway history. (Author's Collection)

Ex-SE&CR L class 4-4-0 number 763 prepares to depart Charing Cross with a train for the Kent coast c.1930. The L class 4-4-0s are often attributed to Richard Maunsell, but were in fact the last design by Robert Surtees, who was the Engineering brains behind Harry Wainwright, who merely took the designs of Surtees and shrouded them in attractive curves. The L class were introduced in 1914, half the class being constructed by Borsig of Berlin and the others being constructed by Beyer Peacock of Manchester. (Author's Collection)

D1 class 4-4-0 tender Locomotive 1747, stands at the head of a passenger train, at Holborn Viaduct station, c 1938. At this time many of the outer commuter train services, operated in mornings and evenings were steam hauled from this and Blackfriars terminal platforms. Full electrification not taking place throughout Kent until 1961, when main line steam services were eliminated. Authors Collection

L1 4-4-0 number 1788 starts out of Cannon Street station, with a commuter train c.1935. This station is the City terminus of the former SE&CR, with services to the Kent coast and parts of East Sussex. During the Second World War, Cannon Street was badly bombed, damaging the overall roof and structure of the building. The roof was taken down in the late 1950s and has now been replaced with an office block, which straddles the platforms.
(Rev Mace, Milepost 92)

Bulleid light Pacific, 21C162 17 *Squadron*, awaits the road, with a Kent coast express c.1947. Here you can see the amount of war time damage that has been done, with the iron structure of the roof devoid of any glass or protection. Later, in the early 1950s, small station canopies and awnings were constructed to provide protection to passengers in bad weather. (Rev Mace, Milepost 92)

Schools class number 927 Clifton departs from Waterloo 13 July 1937; this picture shows how many diagrams the Schools class had from this famous London terminus during the interwar period. Many of the Bournemouth and Weymouth services were rostered to Schools class 4-4-0s and a large number of services on the Portsmouth direct line, via Guildford. (Rev Mace, Milepost 92)

Urie reboilered Drummond D15 4-4-0, number 466 waits at the platform end to work light back to Nine Elms depot, on 13 July 1937. These Locomotives were Drummond's last design, being introduced in 1912, shortly before his death; they had been the main stay of passenger services on the Portsmouth direct line before the Schools class arrived. (Rev Mace, Milepost 92)

Interlude at Waterloo, with Schools class 4-4-0 927 *Repton,* resplendent in its new cote of Bulleid malachite green, with sunshine lettering and a more workmanlike Drummond M7 0-4-4 tank on parcels van duties, in the adjacent platform. The Schools is about to depart for Bournemouth with an express, while the M7 will spend the day pottering around the station, on pilot duties. (Author's Collection)

The Windsor side of Waterloo station, on 1 April 1933, with Ex-SE&CR, F1 4-4-0 number 1074, waiting in the platform with a Reading service, while an electric unit awaits departure to the suburbs. This part of Waterloo station, was always called Old Khartoum and was the only surviving part of the old station, which was rebuilt from the early years of the twentieth century until 1922. The Windsor lines were demolished in the 1990s, to make way for the international station, known as the Eurostar Terminal. (H.C. Casserley)

Branch Lines and Local Services

Quiet day at New Romney, with Ex-SE&CR 01 class 0-6-0 tender goods number 1426, gently simmering in the platform awaiting departure time to Appledore c.1930. The New Romney branch provided an important link with the outside world for farmers and local town's people, who lived on Romney Marsh. The line had a substantial amount of freight, including sheep traffic, which was a feature until the 1950s. The area also became very popular with holiday makers from the 1920s, especially after the 15 inch gauge Romney Hythe & Dymchurch Railway opened in the mid-1920s. (R.C. Stumpf collection)

Another unidentified, 01 class 0-6-0 tender goods runs along the Hythe branch, nearing Saltwood tunnel on its journey to Sandgate, on 10 September 1926. The Hythe branch was originally promoted as an alternative main line along the coast, opened in 1874, to connect Sandling Junction with Folkestone; however, the project was cut back to Sandgate and the connection to Folkestone was never constructed. In 1931, the line was further cut back to Hythe and singled to try to save money, closing to all traffic during the Second World War for three years from 1942 to 1945, finally closing to all traffic on 3 December 1950. The SE&CR operated horse trams between Hythe and Sandgate, to try and improve connections between the branch and the local towns; the trams ceased operating in 1921. (Author's Collection)

Stroudley D1 0-4-2 tank number 2355 propels its motor train of two Ex-LBSCR bogie non corridor carriages, along the Westerham branch on 3 October 1936. The Westerham branch ran from Dunton Green to Westerham and was the branch frequently used by Winston Churchill, when going to and from Chartwell, his country home. After closure in 1961, an attempt was made to preserve the line, but unfortunately the road bed was acquired to become part of the Sevenoaks bypass, now part of the M25. (H.C. Casserley)

Stroudley D1 0-4-2 tank number 2260 and train of Gate Stock, stands in the bay platform at Brookwood awaiting the road for Bisley c.1930. This line, which had extensions to Deepcut during the First World War, only had a train service when there was an event at National Rifle Association or the annual Bisley week. The line was in fact largely owned by the National Rifle Association and maintained under an agreement with the Southern Railway. The branch was extended again to Deepcut in the Second World War and returned to NRA control after the war. The branch finally closed to traffic in 1952, by which time most of the NRA members attended the events by road. (Author's Collection)

Ex-L&SWR Adams T1 0-4-4 tank, number 67, stands with its train at Swanage station, awaiting departure time, to take its train to Wareham on the main line. The Swanage branch was another Southern branch that took holidaymakers to the sea side and local produce to markets in London. The Swanage line also served local industry, in that it transported china clay from the Isle of Purbeck, which was trans-shipped from the clay company's narrow gauge system, into the standard gauge wagons on the branch. (H.C. Casserley)

A post war view of Adams radial 4-4-2 tank, number 3488, waiting in the bay platform at Axminster, with its train of two Ex-L&SWR bogie carriages, to depart for Lyme Regis, on the coast. This branch, like the Wenford Bridge branch had unusual motive power, in the form of three old Adams 4-4-2 radial tanks, the last survivors of a once much larger class of Locomotive, that were originally used on London suburban trains. 3488, had a very interesting history, in that it was sold to the Government in the First World War and then sold again after the war, to the East Kent Railway, where it became their number 5. The Southern Railway only had two Adams radial tanks, for operation on the Lyme Regis branch and it was felt that a third Locomotive was desirable, in case of emergencies. East Kent Railway number 5 was purchased in 1946, to become the third member of the class; however, a twist of fate decreed that this Locomotive was purchased by the Bluebell Railway in 1962, when the Adams radial tanks were withdrawn from service by British Railways. (Author's Collection)

Ex-SE&CR P class 0-6-0 tank, number 178, arrives at Otford, with a service from Sevenoaks, c.1926. This is an example of what the early years of the Southern was like, with old four and six wheel carriage stock on suburban and branch lines, especially in the South Eastern Division, where there was a clear need for investment in new carriage stock. Both the P class tank number 178 and some of this Ex L C & D R, carriage stock have survived and can be still sampled on the Blue Bell Railway in East Sussex. (Author's Collection)

Crystal Palace Low Level station, on 18 February 1928, with LBSCR E5 0-6-2 tank, number 404 on a suburban service and a Brighton overhead electric train in the far right. This was and still is an important transport hub on the South London rail network and during this period, the Brighton overhead electric services were an unusual feature at this location. (H.C. Casserley)

An Ex-L&SWR M7 0-4-4 tank, number 55, hurries south with an outer suburban service through Clapham Cutting c.1925. These long commuter trains of non-corridor bogie stock would often make up trains that operated over the main and New Line to Guildford, or as far as Basingstoke, during this period. (Author's Collection)

One of the unusual features of the Southern in Kent, was the operation of miners' trains, for the Kent coal field. Here we see H class tank number 1016 heading a train of old LC&DR four wheeled carriage stock on such a working, from Margate to Chislet Colliery c.1935. (Rev Mace, Milepost 92)

Another Ex-SE&CR H class 0-4-4 tank number 1161, is seen near Deal, with a train of mixed carriage and parcels van stock, including an LC&DR four wheeled brake and a Maunsell utility van c.1935. (Rev Mace, Milepost 92)

Ex-LBSCR D3 0-4-4 number 2388 tank blows off in the platform at Eastbourne station, after arriving with a local service of two Brighton bogie carriages, making up a motor train set c.1936. These sets were used across the South East, on branches and some suburban operations, lasting in service until British Railways days. (Rev Mace, Milepost 92)

Heavy Freight and Pick up Goods

Maunsell former River class 2-6-4T, rebuilt as a U class 1796, hauls a long heavy freight train near Fleet, on the South Western main line c.1928. Compared with the other big four companies, the Southern had less freight traffic; however, a large tonnage was handled by the South Western Division, which served the West of England and places like Southampton Docks. Here we see a long van train, probably heading for Southampton Docks, which originated at Feltham Yard, where freight trains were marshalled for internal distribution and onward transit to other railways, via the network of connecting lines across London. (R.C. Stumpf collection)

A Bulleid Q 1, 0-6-0 tender goods, number C37, makes light work of a long train of open wagons near Brookwood, in this 1946 picture. The Q1 class was introduced in 1942, to provide extra motive power for the war effort, eventually numbering forty in the class. They were the most powerful 0-6-0 tender goods ever constructed in Britain and were probably the ugliest steam Locomotive ever constructed, with many interesting comments being made when they were introduced. (LCGB Ken Nunn Collection)

One of the impressive Urie H 16 4-6-2 tanks, number 520; these powerful heavy tank Locomotives were introduced in 1921 to work freight traffic across London and within the former L&SWR system. The five members of the class, were largely based at Feltham shed, which served the extensive marshalling yard at that location with its hump shunting facility for making up trains. This picture shows a typical long heavy freight, for which these large tanks were designed, seen here near Virginia Water 1928. (R.C. Stumpf collection)

An Ex-SE&CR 01 0-6-0 tender goods, number 439, heads a long train of cattle wagons, in this early 1920s picture. Although old, the Stirling 0 and rebuilt by Wainwright 01 classes, proved versatile and still useful machines, many of them survived well into British Railways days, the last being withdrawn in 1961. (R.C. Stumpf collection)

Ex-L&SWR Adams B4 0-4-0 T, number 100, on a trip working in Plymouth c.1935, probably heading for the Turnchapel branch, which served an oil depot. A large number of these useful Locomotives were based at Southampton Docks; a given number were also to be found across the former L&SWR system, being used as shunters and pilot Locomotives. (Stephenson Locomotive Society)

Ex-Plymouth Devonport & South Western Junction Railway 0-6-2 T, number 757, Earl of Mountedgecombe, eases a short pick up freight around a curve in Callington goods yard c.1947. The PD&SWJR was one of the lines connected to Col Holman Fred Stephens, who was involved with the lines' construction and fitting out. The independent railway had four Locomotives originally, two Hawthorne Lesley 0-6-2 tanks, a single Hawthorne 0-6-0 tank and a solitary 0-4-2 saddle tank, reconstructed from an 0-4-0 saddle tank, that was originally 3ft 6"gauge. The Hawthorne Leslie products, lasted well into Southern and British Railways days, both the 0-6-2 tanks, not being withdrawn until the late 1950s. (J.H. Aston)

THE HARBOUR, FOLKESTONE

Ships and Docks

Folkestone Harbour in the late 1930s, with a Southern Ferry about to leave harbour for France. The Southern Railway operated a cross Channel steam packet service with first the Nord railway of France and later the nationalised SNCF to Boulogne. Folkestone harbour had been owned by the SE&CR and its predecessor, the South Eastern Railway, since the mid-nineteenth century, when through services to Paris and Europe, were first started by the railways. (Commercial Postcard)

TSS *Isle of Thanet*, which along with her sister ship, Maid of Kent, entered service in 1925. Both ships operated on a number of routes, in their working lives, Isle of Thanet was bombed in Dieppe harbour, on 21 May 1940 but was repaired, not being withdrawn from service until 1964. (Commercial Postcard)

Both the *Isle of Thanet* and the *Maid of Kent,* were constructed by Dennies of Dumbarton, a ship builder who supplied many vessels to the Southern Railway. One of the sisters is shown here leaving Folkestone Harbour in the late 1930s, with a service to Boulogne. (LCGB Ken Nunn Collection)

RMS *Isle of Jersey* was delivered from Dennies of Dumbarton in 1930, along with her sister ship RMS *Isle of Guernsey*, both vessels were requisitioned during the Second World War and served throughout the conflict. After the war both ships re-entered railway service and were not withdrawn until the 1960s. (Commercial Postcard)

The Isle of Wight ferry service had a long association with paddle steamers; here we see the PS *Whippingham*, laid up in the Solent, between operating turns. *Whippingham* and her sister ship, *Southsea*, were constructed by the Fairfield Company in 1930. Both ships were requisitioned in the Second World War, *Southsea* being mined and sunk off the River Tyne on 16 February 1941. *Whippingham* returned from war service to operate the Isle of Wight service until 1963, when she was scrapped. (Pamlin Prints)

PS *Shanklin* steams across the Solent on 20 June 1928, on a service from Ryde to Portsmouth Harbour. Constructed after the First World War, for the joint LBSCR, LSWR shipping service, this vessel, along with the PS Merstone operated the Isle of Wight ferry service throughout the Second World War. PS *Shanklin*, was sold to Cosens in 1951, being renamed *Monarch* and was finally withdrawn in 1961. (Pamlin Prints)

The PS *Ryde* was constructed by Dennies of Dumbarton in 1939, being a sister ship to *Sandown*, constructed in 1934. She was requisitioned for war service during the Second World War, returning to the Southern Railway in 1945. Here we see the paddle steamer steaming across the Solent, on the Portsmouth Harbour to Ryde service c.1947. PS *Ryde* became the last paddle steamer on the Isle of Wight run, not being withdrawn until 1969, when she was sold to become a floating restaurant on the River Medina. (Pamlin Prints)

A general view of the docks at Southampton c.1925, showing four ocean liners at berth and the dock sidings full of wagons awaiting unloading into ships. The Southern Railway inherited Southampton Docks from the L&SWR who in turn had purchased the Southampton Harbour Company, in the late-nineteenth century. Southampton was, and still is, one of the deepest and most important harbours and dock complexes in Britain, with an ability to take some of the world's largest ships. (Commercial Postcard)

The SS *Teutonic* in dry dock in Southampton, c.1925. This picture shows one of the large dry docks at Southampton used to repair and maintain large ocean going ships. Both the L&SWR and the Southern Railway added to the dock complex during their times, which resulted in facilities that became second to none. (Pamlin Prints)

Dock Locomotives and Shunters

The Newhaven Harbour Company was originally an independent concern, later taken over by the LBSCR and becoming part of the Southern Railway in 1923. Although the harbour was owned by the railway, the harbour company remained for many years a separate concern, with its own management. The LBSCR had sold the harbour company a Stroudley Terrier number 72 Fenchurch, for shunting in the docks complex. In Southern Railway days, this Locomotive was taken back into capital stock becoming number 2636 in the list. Here we see the Locomotive in its Newhaven Harbour Company livery, of plain black with yellow lettering outside Newhaven shed c.1923. (Author's Collection)

The Southampton Harbour Company was also an independent concern until taken over by the L&SWR in the late nineteenth century. The harbour company had a fleet of small 0-4-0 saddle tank Locomotives, of which the most modern were a pair of R W Hawthorne 0-4-0 saddle tanks, numbers 734 Clausentum and 3458 Ironside. Both Locomotives survived for many years after the grouping in 1923, Ironside not being withdrawn until the late 1950s. (Photomatic)

Ex-L&SWR Adams B4 class Dinard, on dock shunting duties at Southampton c.1930. These sturdy, strong 0-4-0 tanks, were a feature of Southampton docks for over forty years, only being replaced with the USA class 0-6-0 tanks in the postwar period. Even though most of the B4 tanks were withdrawn and sold after 1946, a small number in good condition continued in traffic until the early 1960s. (Author's Collection)

Ex-L&SWR Drummond C 14 0-4-0 T, number 3741, hauls a two plank open wagon along the tramway at Canute Road Southampton c.1936. These small 0-4-0 tanks were constructed in 1906, as rail motor Locomotives, but were found to be lacking in power, on that work. Between 1913 and 1923 three of the ten members of the class were re built by Robert Urie as 0-4-0 tanks, from their original 2-2-0 wheel arrangement. The other seven were sold to the government for war service, during the First World War. All three survived into British Railways service, the last not being withdrawn until 1958. (R.C. Stumpf collection)

U S Army Transportation Corps 0-6-0 T 4326, during trials at Southampton docks in April 1947, before acceptance by the Southern Railway. Oliver Bulleid had originally intended to design a new class of dock shunter for Southampton in the postwar period, however, it was found that the cheapest and easiest way to replace the old and worn out Adams B4 tanks, was to purchase fourteen US Army surplus 0-6-0 tank Locomotives. These became the Southern's USA class and proved to be a good investment, some remaining in service until the end of Southern Region steam in July 1967. (Author's Collection)

After being taken into stock, the Southern Railway, modified the American constructed Locomotives, with improved cabs, steps and later, a steel plate, on the front buffer beam, to make it safer when cleaning out the Locomotives smoke box. Here we see number 65 in the docks at Southampton, after some modifications had been carried out at Eastleigh Works c.1947. (Author's Collection)

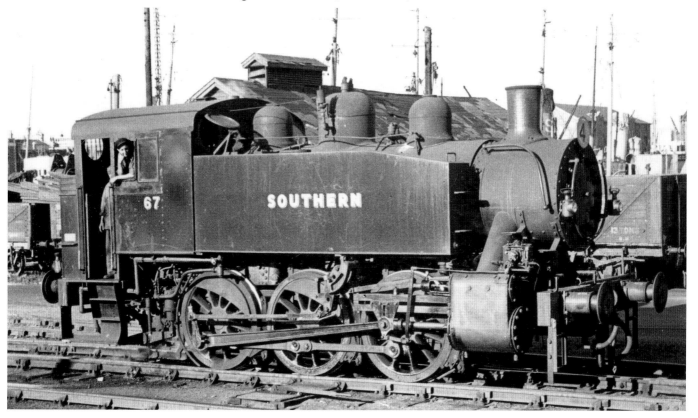

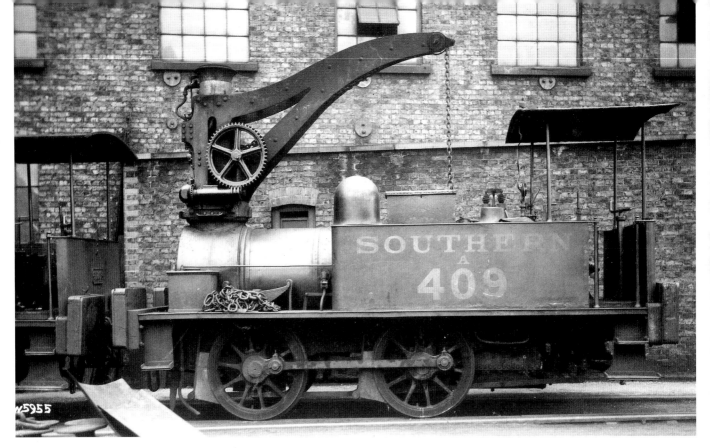

Departmental Locomotives

Ex-SE&CR Neilson-constructed 0-4-0 Crane Tank, number 409, here seen outside Ashford Works c.1930. There were two Neilson crane tanks inherited from the SE&CR in 1923; both machines had originally belonged to the South Eastern Railway and were constructed in 1881. The two machines were long-lived, being taken into British Railways ownership in 1948, but were both withdrawn shortly after nationalisation. (A.C. Roberts)

Manning Wardle constructed 0-4-0 saddle tank number 313, is seen here on a weltrol wagon in transit from Meldon Quarry in North Devon to Eastleigh Works for scrapping on 19 March 1938. This small 0-4-0 saddle tank, was ordered in 1881, by James Stirling for dock shunting at Folkestone Docks, it later gravitated to the Engineers' Department on both the SE&CR and later the Southern. Its last duties were performed at Meldon Quarry, where most of the Southern's granite ballast came from, as their shunting Locomotive, being replaced by a LC&DR T class 0-6-0 tank. (B.W. Anwell)

The Drummond Bug, a 4-2-4 tank inspection Locomotive constructed for Dougal Drummond, C M E of the L&SWR in 1899. This machine covered 171,000 miles in its operational life, largely during Drummond's time, after which it spent long periods in store, as Robert Urie did not like the Locomotive. Its final use was as an inspection Locomotive and saloon for Engineers inspecting the construction of the new docks at Southampton. The Locomotive became number 58S on the Southern's books and was patch painted, having the L and W painted out from its original L&SWR Urie sage green livery and the carriage portion painted in green to match. The Bug was almost saved for preservation, being laid aside in the Eastleigh Works paint shop, along with the last Isle of Wight Railway Beyer Peacock 2-4-0 tank and an L&SWR 0330 class 0-6-0 saddle tank; all three were later scrapped during the Second World War. (Author's Collection)

Isle of Wight Lines

Adams 02 0-4-4 T number 22 Brading heads its train down the pier at Ryde, hauling a train of Ex-L&SWR arch roof carriage stock c.1934. After the grouping in 1923, the Southern railway inherited a mixed bag of lines on the Isle of Wight, including the Isle of Wight Railway, The Isle of Wight Central and the Freshwater Yarmouth & Newport Railway. All the railways taken over were in a bad financial way and needed large amounts of investment, which the newly formed Southern did not have. The answer was to cascade almost new carriage stock from the main land to replace worn out equipment and replace the older Locomotives with surplus motive power from the mainland. (Author's Collection)

Adams 02, number 32 *Bonchurch*, steam escaping from its safety valve, waits in the platform at Newport Station, with its train c.1935. The line from here to Cowes had been the first railway opened on the island, in 1862, later becoming part of the Isle of Wight Central Railway, which opened to Ryde St Jones Road in 1872 and through to Sandown in 1875. The IWCR helped to promote and later took over the Ventnor West Branch, which was opened to traffic in 1900. (Author's Collection)

Cowes station on an autumn day in the mid-1920s, Ex-L&SWR 02 0-4-4 T, number 30, later named *Shorwell*, waits for the road to Newport, with a train of Ex-L&SWR arch roof non corridor stock. As the lines on the island gradually closed, in the 1950s and 1960s, services became more contained, until only the lines from Ryde to Ventnor and Cowes remained, which in turn succumbed to closure in the mid-1960s. Today, only the Isle of Wight Railway remains between Ryde Pier Head and Shanklin and the heritage line to Wootton from Smallbrook Junction. (Author's Collection)

Beyer Peacock 2-4-0 T number W 16 *Wroxall*, stands majestically at Newport, in this portrait taken in the mid-1920s. Long before the 02 0-4-4 tanks appeared on the island in the early 1920s, the Beyer Peacock 2-4-0 tanks were the standard class on the island and were in the majority, both on the Isle of Wight Railway and on the Isle of Wight Central.

As a result of the efforts of A.B. Macleod to improve the motive power and rolling stock situation, on the Islands railways, some newer designs cascaded from the mainland, appeared on the Island's railways, among them were four Stroudley E1 0-6-0 tanks, numbered 1 to 4 and later named. Here we see number 2 *Yarmouth* at Newport shed c.1935; these cascaded Locomotives were used to haul freight and Engineers' trains, but could also be found on some passenger duties, including the Tourist, the only named train on the Island. (R.K. Blencowe)

Ex-LBSCR A1X terrier number 11, *Newport* and train of Stroudley four wheeler carriage stock, stands in the platform at Newport station, with a Freshwater service c.1930. Like the Brighton E1 0-6-0 tanks, A1X Terriers were also supplied to the Isle of Wight system, for use on branch lines and lighter duties, such as shunting and pilot work. All the terriers had returned to the mainland by 1949, the last two being used on the Ventnor West branch. (Author's Collection)

Southern Electric

A train of LBSCR overhead electric stock stands in the platform at Victoria station c.1925. This stock was constructed for the Crystal Palace line and introduced in 1911. The Brighton overhead electric network, which included the South London line from Victoria to London Bridge, via Denmark Hill and the Line to Crystal Palace, opened in stages from 1 December 1909, on the South London line and Victoria, via Streatham Hill to Crystal Palace, from 12 May 1911. The trains ran on a voltage of 750V, AC, using traction motors supplied by Winter Eichberg, of Germany and overhead pick up. The electrification of these suburban lines was intended to be the first stage of a much more ambitious scheme to eventually electrify the main line to Brighton. After the formation of the Southern Railway in 1923, it was decided to standardise on a third rail 660 Volt DC system, which resulted in the Brighton overhead network being converted to third rail. Despite this decision by the Southern, an extension of the overhead system was opened to Coulsdon North and Sutton, which opened as late as 1 April 1925. Later from 1928 onwards the overhead electric lines were converted to third rail DC. This was carried out in stages with the Crystal Palace line, from Victoria, via Streatham Hill being converted on 17 June 1928 and the alternative route to Crystal Palace, being converted on 3 March 1929. The rest of the Brighton overhead electric, over the South London line was converted on 22 September 1929. (Author's Collection)

A three car formation of Crystal Palace stock is seen here near Wandsworth Common on 28 March 1928. The overhead electric trains usually ran in three car sets, which could be lengthened in the rush hour or when required. (H.C. Casserley)

One of the original two car sets, introduced in 1909, stands outside the car sheds at Peckham Rye, c.1922. These sets were plusher and more ornate then the later Crystal Palace sets, having ornate detail in their interiors and finer quality décor. After the conversion of the Brighton Overhead system, these units were converted for reuse as DC sets. (Author's Collection)

One of the power cars constructed for the Coulsdon North extension, which opened in 1925. These power cars could be marshalled inside trains of carriage stock or attached to the end of units, when in service. All of these power cars, were converted to bogie brake vans at Eastleigh after the conversion of the overhead electric. (O.J. Morris)

An Ex-L&SWR three car electric unit number 1201, waits in the platform at Clapham Junction station, with a service to Waterloo c.1924. The L&SWR suburban line from Waterloo to Wimbledon via East Putney was electrified, opening on 25 October 1915; this development heralded the start of what later became the Southern third rail electric network. There were further additions during this time, with services on the Kingston loop and to Shepperton commencing in January 1916 and also extending on the Hounslow loop during March and to Hampton Court in June of that year. Finally, the Guildford new line was electrified to Claygate on 20 November 1916, the rest of the line to Guildford having to wait until 1925. The trains originally used letters for route destinations, V for Waterloo-New Malden-Richmond-Waterloo and so on, there original being eighty-four units in service, when introduced. The carriages were made up of converted 1904 non-corridor steam bogie stock, rebuilt onto timber underframes, with stylish distinctive torpedo style cab fronts. (Author's Collection)

One of the first generation electric units, number 4168 departs Clapham junction, for Claygate c.1946. The trains of electric stock were originally serviced in car depots at Wimbledon, Strawberry Hill and Effingham Junction after steam traction had moved to Feltham. (J.H. Aston)

A 4 Sub unit, number 4547, stands in the platform at Clapham Junction, with a train to Richmond c.1946. The prototype for this class of electric unit number 4101, was introduced in 1941, however production of any further units were put on hold until 1944, when production recommenced with unit 4102. The first production batch of these units started work on suburban services out of Victoria in 1945 and further construction of these units continued after nationalisation in 1948, with steel bodied stock. Note, the Bulleid designed steel bodied carriage next to the leading car, these were often used to strengthen capacity on these suburban workings. (J.H. Aston)

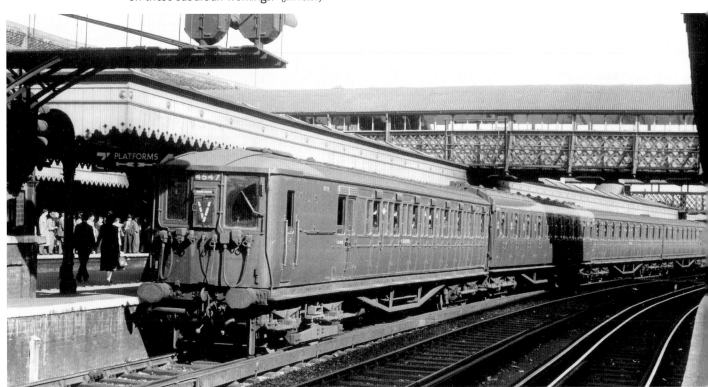

Sub unit number 1749, traverses the junction at Lewisham in the late 1930s, these units were introduced in 1925, for suburban traffic on the newly electrified lines in the London area. Construction of these units continued until the late 1930s and many of them were constructed using former L&SWR and LBSCR carriage stock. These units were finally withdrawn during the 1950s, after sufficient numbers of Bulleid and British Railways electric units had been constructed. (Rev Mace, Milepost 92)

Five Belle unit number 3051 on the quarry line shortly after reintroduction in 1946, these three five-car units were introduced in 1933, for use on the Brighton Belle all-Pullman train. These units continued the tradition of Pullman car services on the Brighton line and were the only all Pullman electric units in the world. The Pullman service was withdrawn during the Second World War, from 1941 to 1946 and returned initially with only two trains, as one set had been damaged at Victoria during the war and had to be rebuilt. The units were finally withdrawn in 1972, having been painted in blue and grey livery for their last years in service. There is a project to reinstate a unit of Brighton Belle stock, for use on the Brighton line and for special rail tours. (Author's Collection)

During 1932, the Southern Railway introduced twenty, six-car main line units, to operate express trains on the lines between London Brighton and West Worthing. These trains had a Pullman car inserted in the set, to facilitate a restaurant service and were classified Six PULL units. Here we see two such units, on the Brighton main line in the mid-1930s, showing how the carriage stock was marshalled.

Six PULL unit 3002, on the quarry line, with an express service c.1938, with Pullman car Rita in its formation. All the units in the Five PULL and six City units had named Pullman cars in their formations.
(Author's Collection)

4 Cor unit, number 3111 at London Bridge in the summer of 1947, its Bulleid Malachite green livery glinting in the sunshine. The 4 Cor units were introduced in 1937 to operate trains on the Portsmouth Direct line, out of Waterloo and the Portsmouth line services via Horsham, out of London Bridge. The units were very popular with the public and long lived in service, not being ousted from main line service until the late 1960s, after which they spent some time in outer suburban and coastal train services, working on the Reading line and also working local trains out of Brighton, along the coast. (J.H. Aston)

Bulleid 4 Sub unit number 4118 in new condition shortly after its construction in 1946, these all steel bodied units had very modern features when constructed in the immediate post war period, including minimalist internal décor and steel framed seating units. These robust and reliable units operated in service until the early 1980s on suburban services on the Southern network in London. (J.H. Aston)

One of six double-ended Dick Kerr units, here seen at Waterloo, on the Waterloo and City Railway in 1940, just before replacement, with the new Bulleid Underground stock. The line originally had a fleet of American-constructed Jackson & Sharp stock, as well as later units by Dick Kerr. The Waterloo and City Railway was opened on 8 August 1898, running from Waterloo to Bank, in the City of London, and was originally an independent electric railway, financially back by the L&SWR, which later took over the concern; in turn it became a part of the Southern in 1923 and by the late 1930s, it became necessary to upgrade the line and replace the by then aged rolling stock. The improvements and replacement of the rolling stock happened during one of the worst periods of the Second World War and shortly after reopening to traffic the line suffered a major setback, when a land mine breached the entrance to Waterloo station, outside the Victory arch, damaging the tunnels of the Waterloo and City Railway. (Southern Railway Official)

Lynton & Barnstaple Railway

The Lynton & Barnstaple Railway, was the Southern's only narrow gauge line; opened in May 1898, it ran from Barnstaple Town station to Lynton and Lynmouth, through some of the finest countryside in North Devon. The line became part of the L&SWR in 1922, as part of the lead up to grouping in 1923, when it became part of the Southern Railway. Unlike the narrow gauge lines owned by the Great Western, the Southern never promoted this gem of a railway and did not know what to do with it. In Engineering terms, the Southern treated it like a main line railway and overspent on unnecessary maintenance, which put up costs. In the late 1920s, a new Locomotive was ordered from Manning Wardle, number 188, Lew and a number of bogie vans and open wagons were also acquired. All of these factors and more resulted in the line being closed in September 1935, followed by a sale of Locomotives and rolling stock, some of it almost new, for scrap. Here we see Locomotive 188 Lew, at the head of a passenger train for Lynton, waiting in the platform at Barnstaple on 17 August 1935. (Rev Mace, Milepost 92)

Locomotive 760 *Exe*, simmers in the sunshine at Barnstaple Town Station, in 1933, with a passenger service for Lynton. The handsome 2-6-2 T Locomotives were all named after rivers and trout streams in the area, all the Locomotives except *Lyn*, an American Baldwin 2-4-2 T, were constructed by Manning Wardle of Leeds. (Rev Mace, Milepost 92)

Locomotive 118 *Lew* again, at Barnstaple Town station in 1933, with a short train of bogie carriage stock. Barnstaple Town was the interchange for the Lynton & Barnstaple line, passengers only having to cross the platform to catch their connection. (Rev Mace, Milepost 92)

2-6-2 T number 760 *Exe*, stands outside Pilton shed in this 1933 picture, awaiting its next turn of duty. Apart from 188 *Lew*, none of these well-maintained narrow gauge Locomotives found a new owner at the sale and were all sold for scrap. (Rev Mace, Milepost 92)

The odd man out, Baldwin Constructed 2-4-2 T, number 762, here seen at Pilton Depot in the early 1920s. This Locomotive was acquired by the railway in 1899, from an American builder, the Baldwin Locomotive works, as a result of the great Locomotive famine, when British builders could not accommodate home orders, as a result of large orders from British overseas railways, especially from India, where large numbers of new Locomotives were being ordered. (Author's Collection)

Locomotive 759, *Yeo*, peeps through the shadows of Pilton Shed in this 1933 picture; in the background one can just see the entrance to the lifting shop, where heavy repairs were carried out. (Rev Mace, Milepost 92)

Locomotive number 762 Lyn, stands at Blackmoor station, after taking water, with a train for Lynton c summer 1934. This was the only American constructed Locomotive on the Southern Railways books at the time and was scrapped a year later in 1935, after the lines closure. Authors Collection

Journeys end; Lynton & Lynmouth station on 17 August 1935, only a month from the line's closure, when thousands of people turned up to ride on the last trains. The railway historian Cuthbert Hamilton Ellis, recounted many years later, how unhelpful the Southern had been about travelling to the Lynton & Barnstaple line in its last week and how the Great Western at Paddington had bent over backwards to get him there. (Rev Mace, Milepost 92)

Southern Named Trains

The Golden Arrow was introduced by the Southern Railway on 15 May 1929, operating an all Pullman train between London Victoria and Dover, which via ferry connected with the Nord, later SNCF, operated Fleche D'Or between Calais and Paris, introduced in 1926. Apart from the war years, the Golden Arrow operated for thirty-seven years, being withdrawn on 30 September 1972. Here we see Bulleid light pacific 21C157 later named *Biggin Hill* heading the famous train near Sandling in 1947. (R.K. Blencowe)

The Brighton Belle, all electric Pullman car train, here seen on the quarry line c1936, the three five car units were the only all electric Pullman car units in the world, they replaced the steam, all Pullman Southern Belle service in 1933. Authors Collection

A look at the Night Ferry, running through the outer London suburbs, in the late 1930s; this picture shows the train formation to good effect and the double headed pair of Maunsell 4-4-0s.
(Rev Mace, Milepost 92)

The all Pullman Devon Belle was introduced on 20 June 1947 and operated from London Waterloo to Ilfracombe in North Devon. The train boasted an observation car, as well as other facilities, which were regarded as luxurious in the immediate post war period. The service waned in the early 1950s, due partly to road competition, as many of its original clientele purchased cars in the 1950s; the service was withdrawn at the end of the 1954 holiday season. Here we see Bulleid light pacific 21C117 *Ilfracombe*, blowing off at Exeter St David's with the Pullman set, bound for London Waterloo in the summer of 1947. (Author's Collection)

Sheds and Workshops

The main erecting shop at Ashford Works, in the mid-1930s, with Ex-SE&CR C class 0-6-0 tender goods number 1691 undergoing repairs and other Locomotive boilers undergoing heavy overhauls on the far left. Ashford was one of the Southern's main overhaul and Locomotive construction facilities, the others being at Brighton and Eastleigh. (Rev Mace, Milepost 92)

On 27 June 1931, Ex-LC&DR T class 0-6-0T number 602 undergoes a heavy overhaul and repaint at Ashford Works. This is an interesting illustration of the organised chaos that seemed to occur when a Locomotive needs to be taken apart, with all the tools and equipment, needed to do the job piled around the Locomotive.
(H.C. Casserley)

Ex-LBSCR Stroudley D 1 0-4-2 T nears the end of a heavy overhaul and repaint in this mid 1930s picture, having just received its coat of the later, lighter shade of Maunsell olive lined green livery. The works at Eastleigh, increasingly found itself overhauling Ex-LBSCR and some ex-SE&CR Locomotives during the 1930s, as Brighton Works was slowly being closed down. The Southern were forced to change their mind over Brighton's closure with the outbreak of the Second World War in September 1939. (R.C. Stumpf collection)

The cavernous space of the main erecting shop at Eastleigh Works, is well illustrated here with large Locomotives being given heavy overhauls under the vast glass and steel roof, c.1946. Here we see an unidentified King Arthur and an H 15, having their boilers attended to, while another Ex-L&SWR Urie 4-6-0 is stripped to its frames. (Rev Mace, Milepost 92)

A post war view of Eastleigh main erecting shop, showing a newly acquired USA tank, number 63, undergoing a heavy overhaul and repaint; note the Locomotive has had its cab modified with side windows and proper cab steps, but has still not had square front cab windows fitted, or a hinged front buffer beam plate, for cleaning out the smoke box. (R.C. Stumpf collection)

Littlehampton Ex-LBSCR shed on 26 February 1927, with an unidentified Stroudley D 1 0-4-2 tank, outside the shed and E3 0-6-2 T number 158, still in its Brighton umber livery, at this time. This is an example of a smaller Ex-LBSCR shed that normally had an allocation of two or three Locomotives, used to work local services and provide motive power for the first and last trains in the day; note the derelict Stroudley four wheel carriage body on the left of the shed, probably used as a Foreman's Office, or mess room. (H.C. Casserley)

The Locomotive shed at Yeovil Town, which belonged to the L&SWR, later Southern, but often hosted Locomotives from the Great Western. Here we see the shed on 12 June 1926, with a selection of interesting Ex-L&SWR Locomotives including Adams Jubilee A12 0-4-2 tender and a number of Drummond small wheeled 4-4-0 s including some K 10 and L 11 types. (H.C. Casserley)

Ex-PD&SWJcR 0-6-2 T number 757, having its wheels and axle journals attended to, at Plymouth Friary shed on 12 July 1924. The Hawthorne constructed Locomotive, is still in Ex-L&SWR livery in this picture; the L&SWR absorbed the PD&SWJcR in 1922, in preparation for the grouping a year later. (H.C. Casserley)

Callington Locomotive depot, in the summer of 1936, with Adams 02 0-4-4 T, number 231, waiting on shed for its next turn of duty. This two road shed had been the main workshops of the PD&SWJcR, before being taken over by the former L&SWR in 1922. (Photomatic)

Two of the three Ex-L&SWR Beattie Well tanks at Wadebridge shed in the late 1920s, with number 0329 leading, with its square splashes and one of the later round splashered machines outside the shed, while an Adams Jubilee A12 0-4-2 tender Locomotive shares its shed road with a line of tank Locomotives. This is an interesting picture, with a good view of the overhead lifting hoist and the timber shed building.
(Author's Collection)

Oil Burning Locomotives

Although the former constituents that later made up the Southern had experimented with oil burning in the pre grouping period, little was done in this direction in the interwar period; however, in 1946 and during 1947, the British Government encouraged the big four railways to invest in oil burning, for its steam Locomotives. Like many schemes dreamed up by politicians, this proved to be a financial disaster, when the price of oil went up and all the money invested in the project was wasted. Here we see Drummond T 9 4-4-0 tender Locomotive, number 114 at Eastleigh, on a local service, waiting to depart, in 1947. This is a good illustration of the tender arrangements of an oil burning Locomotive, showing the way the oil tank is fitted and its refuelling arrangements, on the top. (Lens of Sutton Collection)

Maunsell N class 2-6-0 1831, in wartime black livery, is also a converted oil burning Locomotive, here seen at Eastleigh in the summer of 1947. The Locomotives that took part in this oil burning fiasco were varied, in that both modern machines like the N class and even at least one Bulleid light pacific were involved; also older Drummond 4-4-0s and a solitary A1X terrier number 515S, were converted. (Author's Collection)

Petrol and Diesel Locomotives

A petrol tractor which was constructed by the Southern Railway, in the 1920s, for light shunting around Eastleigh Works. This four wheeled machine was mostly used around the carriage and wagon works and lasted in use for many years. (Author's Collection)

Fowler 0-4-0 Diesel Mechanical shunter number 400S was acquired by the Southern to operate on Engineers trains in Southampton docks. Here we see the Locomotive at the Engineers store and workshops, in the docks c.1947. (Author's Collection)

The prototype Maunsell 350 HP 0-6-0 Diesel Mechanical shunter number 1, here seen in a works picture taken in 1937, when it was introduced. The three 0-6-0 Diesel Mechanical shunters were constructed by English Electric for the Southern Railway, for use at Norwood Yard and Hither Green. During the Second World War, all three were requisitioned by the War Department for use on the South Coast near Dover, to move and place heavy railway guns, being used to bombard the French coast. All three survived into British Railways days, being withdrawn in the early 1960s. (R.C. Stumpf collection)

Maunsell Diesel Mechanical shunter number 3, here seen engaged in shunting coal wagons in a coal yard in South London, c.1939. (Author's Collection)

Absorbed Steam Locomotive Classes

Ex-SE&CR D class 4-4-0 Tender Locomotive number 75, is seen here heading a passenger train through Kent in early Southern days c.1924. The Wainwright D class 4-4-0s were some of the most handsome pre-grouping express passenger Locomotives ever to run in Britain. Here we see number 75 in its early dark olive, Southern Maunsell livery, still with SE&CR cast iron cab side plates; these were being removed by the mid-1920s. (R.C. Stumpf collection)

Ex-SE&CR Stirling R class 0-6-0 T, number 70, here seen in original condition, with rounded cab and domeless boiler mounted safety valve. These robust, reliable 0-6-0 tank Locomotives, had long lives and were the mainstay of motive power on the Canterbury & Whitstable Railway and on the Folkestone Harbour branch, until the late 1950s. (Author's Collection)

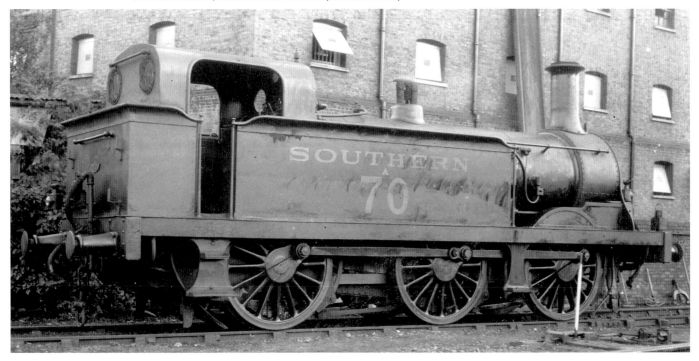

James Stirling designed some fine, long lived classes of steam Locomotive for the South Eastern Railway, later SE&CR; here we see 0 class number 376 on shed awaiting its next turn of duty c 1925. Not all of these venerable 0-6-0 tender goods Locomotives were rebuilt during Wainwright's time, to become 01 class and as we can see from this picture, despite their age, a number found a further lease of life after grouping, for a few years on the newly formed Southern. (Author's Collection)

A pair of SE&CR Locomotives, prototype L C & D R, T class 0-6-0 T number 600, later sold into industrial service and F 1 4-4-0 tender express Locomotive number 450 stand in the yard at Longhedge in South London on 1 June 1929. (H.C. Casserley)

Saddle tank Locomotive number 1685 was originally a Wainwright C class 0-6-0 tender goods, before being re built by Richard Maunsell into its tank configuration, for use at Bricklayers' Arms depot. Here we see the Locomotive in the early 1930s in the yard at Bricklayers' Arms, between shunting turns. (Author's Collection)

Wainwright J class 0-6-4 tank number 1596, on a suburban train at Rochester c.1936, painted in the later lined Maunsell light olive green. The five members of this class of outer suburban tank Locomotives were not totally successful, having the same size boilers as the Wainwright H class 0-4-4 tanks. However, even though they were under-boilered, they lasted in service until the early 1950s, long enough to be painted in lined mixed traffic black by British Railways. (R.C. Stumpf collection)

Stirling, Wainwright re boilered F1 class 4-4-0 tender Locomotive number 1249; often referred to as Flying Bedsteads, these distinctive machines were to be found on semi-fast and local services on the South Eastern Division throughout the whole of the Southern Railway period and were not finally withdrawn until the mid-1950s, under British Railways. (Photomatic)

A pair of Stroudley Ex-LBSCR B1 class 0-4-2 tender Locomotives, numbers 172 and 197, wait outside Brighton station in the late 1920s, resplendent in their lined olive green livery. Both these Locomotives were withdrawn with the other members of the class in the early 1930s, number 197 being withdrawn in August 1932 and 172 going in September 1933. Today the only survivor of the Stroudley express passenger classes, is *Gladstone*, on display at the National Railway Museum at York. (Author's Collection)

The LBSCR constructed a war memorial Locomotive after the First World War, this being Locomotive number 333 Remembrance, later renumbered 2333 as seen here on shed c.1932. These large, impressive-looking Baltic 4-6-4 Tanks were used on the fast London to Brighton and Eastbourne expresses, until the electrification of both lines in the mid-1930s, the Baltic tanks being taken off the Brighton services in 1933 and a year later from the Eastbourne services. All the Baltic tanks were rebuilt by Maunsell into 4-6-0 tender Locomotives, becoming class N 15X and finding a new life until the mid-1950s, on the South Western Division. (Author's Collection)

Ex-LBSCR Billington E4X 0-6-2T number 485 here seen at Brighton Locomotive shed in the early 1930s. These Locomotives were re built by D. Earl Marsh in the 1900s into the form seen here, with superheating and an extended smoke box. The class was used on outer suburban and semi fast passenger services when introduced in 1897; however, they were equally good on freight work, which made them a useful all round design. The last members of the class were not withdrawn until the early 1960s, Birch Grove being the only survivor on the Bluebell Railway, in East Sussex. (Author's Collection)

Probably one of the most attractive mixed traffic Locomotives ever constructed, the LBSCR K class 2-6-0 tender Locomotive, designed by L W Billington, the last Chief Mechanical Engineer of the LBSCR and introduced in 1913, these useful mixed traffic Locomotives were not withdrawn until 1962; sadly none were preserved. (Author's Collection)

Adams T3 4-4-0 tender Locomotive number 571 stands on Eastleigh shed c.1928. These classic L&SWR main line passenger Locomotives were some of the most graceful-looking late Victorian machines ever constructed. They were very successful on the top link turns; they were assigned to and lasted in traffic on secondary services until the end of the 1930s. The last three members of the class were not withdrawn until after the Second World War and luckily one survives in the National Collection. (Photomatic)

Adams Jubilee A12 class 0-4-2 tender Locomotive number 544 looks handsome in its lined olive green, in this early 1930s picture. These fine Locomotives hauled the most important expresses on the L&SWR when they were introduced in 1887 and were named Jubilee class in honour of Queen Victoria's fiftieth anniversary on the throne. They continued to be good useful Locomotives well into Southern days and the last was not withdrawn until 1948, along with the final member of the Adams T1 class 0-4-4 T, which used the same boiler, known as Jubilee tanks. (Author's Collection)

Ex-L&SWR 0330 class 0-6-0ST number 0328, shunts at Clapham Yard c.1925; a number of these Beyer Peacock designed tanks survived well into Southern railway days, being used on shunting duties and piolet work. This class was not only constructed for use in Britain, but also found favour in Sweden, where a good number of them worked on the state railways, doing the same work. The Southern exchanged a member of this class, number 0334, with the Kent & East Sussex Railway, for their Hawthorne-constructed 0-8-0T, number 4 Hecate, which after overhaul worked out of Nine Elms on Clapham Yard shunting duties. (Author's Collection)

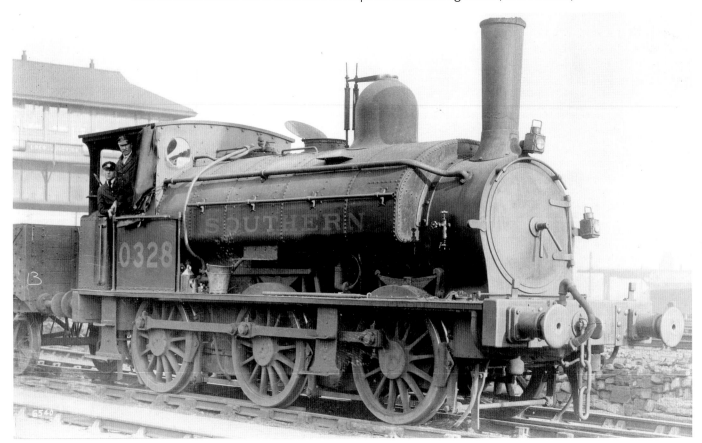

Robert Urie-designed G16 4-8-0T number 493, introduced in July 1921; these powerful tank Locomotives were constructed to be used as hump shunters at Feltham marshalling yard. They occasionally managed to escape the yard on trip workings and heavy cross London freights, but normally spent their time in the yard, shunting and working lines of wagons over the humps. All four members of the class were withdrawn from service during 1962, along with the five Urie H 16 4-6-2 tanks. (Photomatic)

Southern Inter-Regional Trains

Ex-L&SWR rebuilt Drummond T14 4-6-0 tender locomotive number 443, runs through Neasden with a cross London freight, on 23 June 1948. These 4-6-0s were rebuilt three times in their working lives, firstly being reboilered by Robert Urie, then secondly having their paddle box splashes removed by Richard Maunsell and lastly being modified and receiving new chimneys by Oliver Bulleid. One member of the class was destroyed during the war, when it was the victim of a direct hit at Nine Elms shed, during an air raid, but all the other class members lasted into British Railways days, the last being withdrawn in 1951. (H.C. Casserley)

D1 4-4-0 Tender Locomotive 1743, coasts into Kensington Addison Road station, with a train of L M S carriage stock, making up The Sunny South Express on the 26th August 1933. This train dated back to L B S C R days, connecting the north of England with the holiday resorts on the former Brighton network. The train in the picture is made up of L N W R and Midland Railway bogie carriage stock, making up a ten vehicle formation. H C Casserley

An unidentified Maunsell mogul arrives with an inter-regional train from Reading, heading for the north, while a Great Western 28XX 2-8-0 heavy freight Locomotive stands in the goods yard at Oxford in the summer of 1949. (Rev Mace, Milepost 92)

Bridges and Viaducts

A Wainwright C 0-6-0 tender goods crosses Eynsford Viaduct, with a down freight, in the mid-1930s; this is a fine photograph of this imposing structure framed by the trees on a summers day. (Rev Mace, Milepost 92)

E5 X number 2401 crosses the swing bridge near Shoreham, on the line from Brighton to Portsmouth, with a train of Maunsell corridor stock c.1936. (Author's Collection)

Ex-L&SWR Adams 02, 0-4-4T, number 233, heads a train of Gate Stock, across the bridge at Plymouth on the Turnchapel branch, on 14 June 1926. (R.C. Casserley)

The steel girder bridge, across the Camel estuary, on the line to Padstow, on 28 May 1950. This bridge is still in situ and is now part of the Camel trail, a walking and cycling trail from Padstow to Bodmin, in Cornwall. This former L&SWR line, was closed in 1966 to passenger traffic, but remained open to freight for a further decade. (J.H. Aston)

Calstock Viaduct, on the former PD&SWJcR; this impressive viaduct was constructed to cross the River Tamar on the line to Gunnislake and Callington, and is here seen on 27 June 1956. The Engineering for the PD&SWJcR was supervised by Lt Col Holman Fred Stephens, the well-known light railway Engineer and promoter. Part of the line used the track bed of the 3ft 6in gauge, East Cornwall Mineral Railway, a narrow gauge line that served mines in the area. Calstock viaduct is still in use today and is part of the Gunnislake branch on the Tamar Trail. (J.H. Aston)

The Plymouth portion of the 2.50 service to Waterloo crosses the viaduct at Meldon on 6 July 1948, headed by a Great Western Churchward Mogul. Meldon viaduct is made up of two structures, constructed side by side and was the highest point on the Southern Railway. The first single track viaduct was constructed and opened on 12 October 1874 and the second line was completed in 1878. The viaduct was in use until the 1990s, as a headshunt for trains of ballast from Meldon quarry; however, because of fears over the viaduct's structural integrity in the 1990s, the single line used by quarry trains was lifted and the viaduct is now only used by walkers. Meldon Viaduct is an important railway structure and is now listed as an historic transport site. (J.H. Aston)

Unusual Carriage Stock

Former LC&DR six wheeler carriage, converted for use as a holiday camping coach in the 1930s. This vehicle was number 1 in the future fleet and was photographed for publicity purposes. (Southern Railway Official)

The experimental Sentinel Steam rail car, purchased by the Southern Railway in 1933 and used on a number of branches, to assess the possibility of cutting operating costs. Although the steam rail car was widely tested on various lines, it did not meet the expectations of the operating department and was put into store in 1939, when the Second World War broke out. It was broken up in the late 1940s after being used as a mess room at Ashford works, for fire watchers during the war, here seen at Devil's Dyke station, c.1934. (Author's Collection)

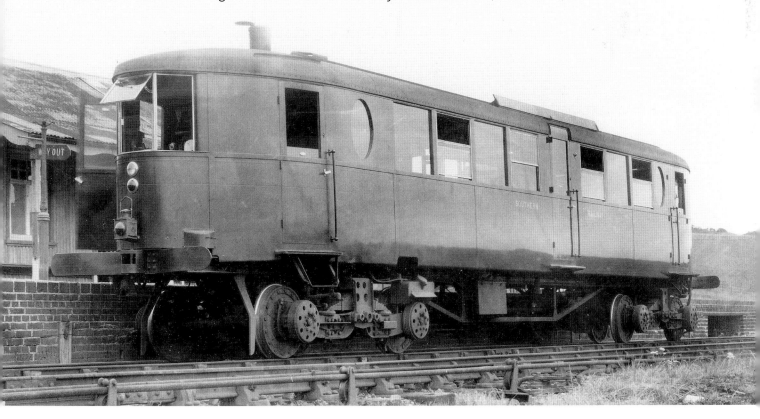

The Southern At War

Charing Cross station, after a heavy air raid on 8 October 1940, when forty-eight people were killed or injured. This station sustained damage on a number of occasions during the Second World War, including a parachute mine becoming entangled with girders of Hungerford Bridge and serious damage from a V1 attack in 1944. (Southern Railway Official)

Bomb damage after an air raid on Victoria, in the London blitz, showing the extensive damage caused after bombs dropped on the carriage sheds to the south of the station, near Grosvenor Bridge, on 7 September 1940. (Southern Railway Official)

The remains of T 14, number 458, after an air raid at Nine Elms Locomotive sheds, on 30 September 1940. This was the first member of the T14 class to be withdrawn as a result of damage, which was not economic to repair. (Southern Railway Official)

E1 4-4-0 tender Locomotive number 1497, being recovered from the aftermath of an air raid at Peckham Rye, on 20 April 1941. The Locomotive has luckily escaped severe damage and is being quickly hoisted back on to the track, for transport to works for repair. (Southern Railway Official)

A Selection of Stations

Bromley North Station, shortly after its refurbishment in the 1920s, showing the Southern's new look, in station architecture, with its plain reserved, brick and stone finish. This style later gave way to the interwar, Walker period concrete and steel architecture we associate with the company. (Commerial Postcard)

Upper Sydenham station on the branch to Crystal Palace on 13 July 1954, showing the interesting arrangement for the foot bridge, near the tunnel mouth. (H.C. Casserley)

The stark concrete platform and waiting shelter of Chevening Halt, on the Westerham branch, here seen in 1960. The Southern will always be remembered for its concrete structures and civil Engineering; most of the concrete parts were manufactured at Exmouth Concrete Works near Exeter and delivered in kit form, for assembly on site. (Lens of Sutton Association)

Rochester station was a good example of former SE&CR and Southern architecture from the interwar period; here we see the pre grouping station buildings on the right and later Southern additions on the left, with its steel and brick buildings. (Author's Collection)

Allhallows-on-Sea, was the terminus for the Allhallows branch, which opened on 16 May 1932 and closed on 4 December 1961. The station was quite substantial for a branch of this kind and the Southern had high hopes of the branch being a success; however, things turned out very differently. The line was promoted as the Southern's new seaside resort on the muddy shores of the Thames estuary. Everyone went to Allhallows once and never came back; the railway promoted the location as if it was a wonderful place for a holiday, but the public took a very different view, regarding it as a rotten place for a week's holiday, with almost no amenities or amusements. (Lens of Sutton Association)

Appledore, Ex-SE&CR, was the junction for the New Romney branch, which was and as far as Dungeness still is a branch line off the Hastings to Ashford line. Here we see the station on 25 April 1947, in the last year of the Southern Railway, with a C class 0-6-0 tender goods outside the goods shed, probably waiting to run light to Ashford or down the branch for its next turn of duty. (H.C. Casserley)

Kemp Town station, Ex-LBSCR, was the terminus of the Kemp Town branch a line that served a suburb of Brighton, opened in 1869 and was successful, until tram competition took away the traffic. The line continued as a passenger and freight operation, until 1932, when the Southern withdrew the passenger service and operated the branch as a freight only line. The line finally closed to traffic in 1971, by which time only coal traffic was left. We see the station buildings after closure to passengers in October 1949. (Tom Middlemass)

Rudgewick station, on the Ex-LBSCR Guildford to Horsham line, with a pick up goods, headed by a Billington C2X 0-6-0 tender goods, arriving to shunt the goods yard c.1947. This branch was opened in October 1865, to provide the LBSCR with a line to access lucrative traffic from Guildford and the Portsmouth main line. The line was a success until bus competition in the interwar period made inroads into the lines passenger traffic profits. By the 1960s, the line had become a backwater, apart from the traffic between Guildford and Cranleigh, which was still lucrative. Despite the potential for keeping the line open as far as Cranleigh, for passenger services from Guildford, there was a determination to close the line by British Railways management, which they did on 14 June 1965, only four months before the line's centenary. (Author's Collection)

Aldershot station, in the interwar period, with an Adams Jubilee A12, 0-4-2 tender Locomotive heading a military troop train in the platform, which includes a horsebox. This station is the junction for the lines to Guildford, also south to Alton through to Winchester and had a service through to Portsmouth via Fareham at this time. Aldershot also had services over the former SE&CR to Reading and over the former L&SWR to Ascot. This station still acts as an important junction station, however the line through to Winchester now only exists as far as Alresford, on the Mid Hants heritage railway and the Meon Valley line, from Alton to Fareham was closed in 1955. (D. Thompson)

Bentley station, on the line from Aldershot to Alton, was the junction for the Bordon branch; here we see a local service headed by Jubilee A12 0-4-2 Tender Locomotive number 632, while a Drummond M7 0-4-4T waits for any passengers, in the Borden branch bay platform C 1930. Opened in December 1905, the Bordon branch served the military at Bordon camp, the line operated a passenger and freight service until September 1957, when passenger services ceased, freight followed in April 1966, with the running down of the Longmoor Military Railway, which closed in 1971. (Author's Collection)

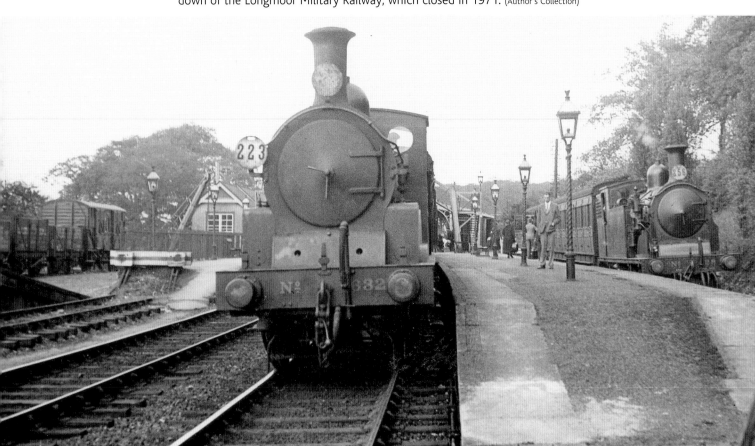

Basingstoke station in the 1920s; this former L&SWR station was an important junction for lines to Bournemouth, Weymouth and the West Country, via Salisbury and the Great Western line via Reading. The station also had important national connections via Reading, to the Midlands, Wales and the North of England. Originally, Basingstoke had a separate Great Western station, which closed in the 1930s, when like Salisbury, the Southern station master, was placed in charge of Southern and Great Western services. The bay platform on the far right, was the platform for the Basingstoke and Alton Light Railway, which opened in 1900 and finally closed in 1936, a line that was owned by the L&SWR and constructed as a blocking line to prevent the Great Western from expanding any further south into L&SWR territory.
(Commercial Postcard)

Lymington Pier, in the mid-1930s, with a Drummond M7 0-4-4T and train waiting for passengers off the Isle of Wight ferry. The branch connects Brockenhurst with Lymington Town and Pier, opening in May 1858, later becoming part of the L&SWR. Services from here were worked by railway owned and Red Funnel-owned ships, at different periods; here we see what appears to be Red Funnel-owned ship at the pier. This was the last branch in the South of England to have steam traction, which came to an end in 1966, when the branch was electrified. (Author's Collection)

Oakhampton station, c.1960, showing the 1930s constructed Walker period buildings, with their brick and steel features. Oakhampton was an important transport hub in this area of North Devon, having lines that connected with Exeter, Plymouth, through to the Bude and Padstowe lines in North Cornwall. Also, Meldon Quarry and Viaduct are located a mile to the west of this station, the quarry providing most of the granite track ballast for the Southern railway and later British Railways, Southern Region. Oakhampton closed to passengers in 1972, but the line through the station remained open for quarry traffic, which continued until the recent years. This station still exists and has a limited train service on weekends in the summer months; however the quarry traffic has ceased owing to the quarry being mothballed. (Lens of Sutton Association)

Tavistock North station on the former L&SWR line to Plymouth, on 27 July 1931, showing the buildings and footbridge. The L&SWR line through to Plymouth opened in 1877 and gave an alternative route to the Great Western main line. Tavistock North station, opened in 1908 and was originally part of the Plymouth Davenport & South Western Junction Railway. There were two stations in Tavistock, one being the original South Devon station, later Great Western and the PD&SWJcR station, on the Plymouth line. The former Southern route was handed over to the Western Region of British Railways in 1963 and closed to traffic in 1968. In Southern Railway days, a portion of the Atlantic Coast Express ran on this section from London Waterloo and the station enjoyed a good connecting service to most parts of the South Western division. (Lens of Sutton Association)

Dunsbear, on the North Devon & Cornwall Junction Railway, here seen on 8 June 1959. The ND&CJcR was a line promoted to connect two sections of the former L&SWR, from Torrington to Halwill Junction and was engineered by Lt Col Holman Fred Stephens, the famous light railway promoter and engineer. The line served a largely rural community, however one of its main sources of revenue was derived from the ball clay industry at Marland. The line had substantial buildings and structures along its formation, including several steel bridges and station buildings constructed of local stone. The line made little money from its passenger service, so inevitably it closed in March 1965, ball clay traffic continuing on the northern part of the line, from Meeth to Marland, until August 1982. (J.H. Aston)

Southern Horsepower

The Southern Railway operated a large number of horses, which were used on road delivery services, here we see a horse and wagon delivering goods in the streets of Guildford c.1925. (E. Jackson)

The Southern also used horses in goods yards and here we see one being used to shunt wagons in the mid-1930s at Shoreham in West Sussex. (Author's Collection)

The Bulleid Leader Locomotive

In the last years of the Southern Railway, Oliver Bulleid started a project to construct a class of revolutionary new steam Locomotives with new features, including sleeve valves. These machines were intended to replace the M7 0-4-4T Locomotives, however problems arose, as a result of the materials available just after the Second World War and having to rush the project before nationalisation took place. An experimental Locomotive, or Guinea Pig, was necessary to test the sleeve valves. The Locomotive used for this was Ex-LBSCR, H1 Atlantic number 2039, *Hartland Point,* which is seen here at Brighton works, as renumbered 32039, in between running sessions c.1949. The sleeve valves worked well on this Marsh designed Atlantic, dating from the 1900s; however, there were lots of problems with the first prototype Leader Locomotive, which kept damaging its sleeve valves due to vibration. (Author's Collection)

Little and Large, prototype Leader bogie Locomotive number 36001, in works grey, being towed outside Brighton Works, by the works shunter A1X Terrier, number 377S, formally 2635. The Leader, referred to by enginemen as the Chinese Laundry, was hell to work on, with a confined space for the fireman, who could not communicate with the driver. The only ventilation while firing was through a small window, as the machine had been designed to burn oil. In all, five Leaders were started, but only two were completed, 36001 and 36002, of which only the first ever steamed. Both the completed Locomotives and the parts of the other three, which were rolling chassis, were stored at New Cross shed and later quietly broken up for scrap. (R.C. Stumpf collection)

Nationalisation 1948

War time black, S15 number S828, still largely in Southern Railway livery, is showing signs of transition, with its S number and British Railways in Bulleid style sunshine lettering. Here seen on a freight in the summer of 1948 near Winchfield, heading south towards Basingstoke. (E.C. Griffith)

I3 4-4-2T, number 32027, storms through Wandsworth common with a train of empty carriage stock, on 25 February 1950. Despite the two years and two months since nationalisation, this Locomotive is still in Southern livery, except its number and the fitting of a Smoke Box Number Plate. (Pamlin Prints)

This is probably one of the strangest things to come out of nationalisation in 1948; someone really got it wrong about the 30,000 number. I do not think Schools class, 30903 *Charterhouse*, ran in public like this, but it might have been an Oliver Bulleid joke; he was not a fan of nationalisation, calling 222 Marylebone Road, British Railways headquarters, the Kremlin.
(Lens of Sutton Association)

The prototype Lord Nelson Class, number 30850 *Lord Nelson*, here seen at Eastleigh Depot on the 25th March 1950. This is a good example of a Southern Locomotive in transition, still in malachite lined green, but now fitted with a smoke box number plate and lettered in early British Railways lettering. This Locomotive is now part of the National Collection and is currently in working order, on the Mid Hants Railway. A B Hurst

Bulleid light pacific 34006 *Bude*, during the Locomotive exchanges, arriving at Marylebone station on a train from Nottingham Victoria in 1948. Both Merchant Navy and Light Pacifics took part in the Locomotive exchanges acquitting themselves well, on all the regions to which they were loaned. (A. Gosling)